one hundred
*More Wisdom
Stories*

For Isabella Rose,
whose life story is just beginning.
May it be a story guided by wisdom
and overflowing with love.

one hundred

More Wisdom Stories

compiled by

MARGARET SILF

LION

Published by Lion Books
an imprint of
Lion Hudson plc
Wilkinson House, Jordan Hill Road,
Oxford OX2 8DR, England
www.lionhudson.com/lion

ISBN 978 0 7459 5606 0
e-ISBN 978 0 7459 5757 9

First edition 2013

A catalogue record for this book is available from the British Library

Contents

LIFE LESSONS

Introduction

Everyone loves a story. The best stories have a life of their own. They get inside us and have the power to change us.

We hear stories every day, on television, on the internet, in the newspapers. Some of them inspire us, but many of them leave us discouraged and anxious. If they change us at all, they may even harden our hearts, and tempt us to curl up more and more tightly in our comfort zone.

This book is a collection of stories of a rather different kind. These are stories to coax us *out* of the comfort zone, and risk the changes that can happen in our hearts when we take this risk. They may inspire us, warn us, challenge us. They may melt our hearts or strengthen our resolve. They may encourage us, giving us hope where we saw only despair. They may make us laugh. They may make us cry. But they will not leave us untouched. They may evoke memories or provoke questions. They won't provide ready-made answers, but they may leave us with the feeling that we have just discovered afresh what was always there inside us.

Stories are full of paradox. We tell our children stories to help them settle at bedtime. Yet those same stories also have the power to *unsettle* us. Stories that calm us one day may disturb us the next. Stories can comfort those parts of us that need a tender touch, and disturb those parts of us that need a wake-up call. But they do their work gently, nudging us over the edge of new possibilities when, and only when, we are ready to embrace their invitation.

How we receive them is up to us. We can hear them as children, and then go back to sleep. Or we can hear them with adult ears, and respond to their call to wake to something new. Or, put another way, we can hear them with children's ears, alert and eager to discover where they are leading us – or with adult minds, already solidly set into adult mindsets, going nowhere. They are what they are. How we respond to them lies in our own free choice.

The call of the story is a call to the heart, where truths that lie deeper than the literal and the cerebral are glimpsed. Follow that call as far as you will, and, above all, enjoy the journey.

A heartfelt word of thanks...

Most of these stories were written or gathered while I was living in Calgary, Alberta, as writer-in-residence at the FCJ Christian Life Centre throughout the autumn of 2012. I would like to express my very warmest gratitude to Mary Robertson, Director of the Centre, for making this possible and for keeping me supplied with wisdom and encouragement, muffins and mirth. My heartfelt thanks also go to the Sisters, Faithful Companions of Jesus, for so generously sharing their home and their hearts with me, as well as allowing me to read them the stories, fresh from the laptop, after our evening meals. Thank you also to the "Stirring the Waters" writers' group for making me so welcome in their circle, and to all who inspired me during my stay in Canada. Very special thanks go to Joyce and Colin Campbell in Toronto for the gift of a friendship that spans the years and the oceans.

The Ways
of God

1

Finding God

One day a little boy decided to go and look for God. He set off after breakfast and headed for the nearby park. He was only a small boy, with short legs, and by the time he reached the park it was time for a snack.

He sat down on a bench and got out his sandwiches and lemonade. Soon an elderly lady came and sat down on the bench beside him. She looked tired, and the little boy was sorry for her and offered her some of his lunch. She accepted his kindness with a grateful smile.

After lunch the two of them sat on the bench and chatted together. The boy told the woman about his family and his school and his hopes and dreams for the future, and the more he told her, the younger the woman felt, and the more inspired and energized. She in her turn listened to his story with a loving, knowing smile, and told him a few stories of her own.

When the little boy got back home, his mother asked him, "So, did you find God?"

"Oh, yes," he replied without hesitation. "And she has the most amazing smile."

And that evening the old lady told her husband of her day's encounter. "I met God in the park today," she said, "and he is much younger than I expected."

Source unknown

Count the stars

There was once a young girl who had a secret dream. She longed to be able to look into the eye of God. One day she confided her longing to a wise old man, who told her the secret.

"If you want to look into the eye of God, you must begin to count the stars, starting with the middle star of Orion's belt, and counting towards the east. Don't count any star twice, and don't miss any. When you reach the 10,000th star you will be looking into the light of God's eye."

So night after night, week after week, month after month, the girl counted the stars, not missing any and not counting any star twice. Eventually she was nearing the end: 9,998… 9,999… And as she reached the 10,000th star, she realized that it was the very same star with which she had begun, the middle star of Orion's belt. Through the year the constellations had rotated through 360 degrees. She was surely gazing into the light of God's eye. She was overjoyed.

She ran to tell the wise old man, and he told her the meaning of her marathon star count.

"You see," he explained, "when you began you couldn't recognize what was right in front of you all the time. So God moved heaven and earth to bring you to this moment."

She gazed again at the heavens, and, as she did so, the star twinkled back to her – the middle star of Orion's belt, the first star and the last, and God smiled: "See how much I love you."

Retelling of a story by Megan McKenna and Tony Cowan

3

Island chapel

There was once a beautiful island. The islanders would walk along its shores every day. They listened to the waves crashing. They caught the wind in their faces. They tasted the salty tang in the air. They felt the sand between their toes, watched the seabirds soaring and swooping, and heard the breeze rustling through the trees.

They were so overawed by the beauty of their island home that they felt a deep desire to praise and worship its creator. So they built a little chapel in the middle of the island. But when they went inside their chapel, they were sad to notice that they could no longer hear the waves or the rustling of the wind, or see the seabirds wheeling, or taste the salty air or feel the kiss of the breeze or the caress of the sand between their toes.

To try to make up for this loss, they filled the chapel with their own words and songs in an attempt to recapture the magic of the mystery. But they disagreed about which words, which songs to use. Once united in community, they began to fragment into opposing factions. Gradually more and more of them stopped going into the little chapel because they didn't find the creator's spirit there.

One little girl, however, kept on coming back, to sit there in the silence and the stillness. Years passed and she became a wise old woman. Every day she rejoiced in the wind and the waves of her island home and every day she spent a quiet half-hour in the chapel. People began to ask her why she did this.

"Well," she explained, "if I listen carefully to the deep stillness there in the chapel, I hear the wind and the waves, the seagulls and the trees, right inside my heart, where they can never fade or die, and the creator spirit invites me to take a walk inside my soul. And the spirit seems to whisper: 'Outside, inside, I am everywhere: beyond you, within you, beside you, above you, below you, around you. There is nowhere that I am not. Be at home in me.'"

Margaret Silf

4

Circular God

There was a heated debate going on at the theological conference. Learned scholars were arguing over whether human beings really contain a spark of God.

Some declared that there is that of God in everyone, while others insisted that only those who believed certain things could be saved.

Some said that it was supremely important to belong to a particular religious group and to hold to the tenets of that group and defend them rigorously. Others were more open in their understanding, and declared that no one group could ever hold the complete truth.

Finally, a young man, whom hardly anyone knew and who had never written any books or been ordained in any church, stood up and told them about an ancient philosopher called Empedocles, who had lived six centuries before Christ, and who had asserted: "God is a circle, whose centre is everywhere and whose circumference is nowhere."

There was a stunned silence in the auditorium. Then they began to murmur and demand that the young man explain himself.

"Well," he said, "I think this means that God is in every particle of creation, and in every human heart. Therefore God's centre is simply everywhere. And God's circumference is nowhere, because there is no edge to divinity. It is impossible to be outside the circle. When we draw circles that include some people and exclude others we are not being true to the divine intention."

And with this the conference adjourned for lunch.

Margaret Silf

5

Paradise found

There was once a very discontented man, who wanted to discover the way to paradise but had so far had no luck. One day, after listening to the wisdom teacher talking about paradise, he decided to set off to find it.

It was a long trek. By the end of a long day's walk he seemed to be no closer than he had been at the start.

When night fell he lay down to sleep, but, fearful that he would not remember in the morning which direction he had been heading in, he placed his shoes pointing in the right onward direction.

But in the night the trickster came by, and turned the man's shoes right round to point in the opposite direction.

When the man awoke, he put on his shoes, having noted the direction they were indicating, and set off again. Another long day's walk followed, and by nightfall he arrived at what had to be paradise. But it looked strangely familiar. It looked just like his own village. It looked just like his own house. And, sure enough, there was his wife, cooking dinner for them both. And he realized that he had discovered what he had set out to find, and they both lived happily ever after.

Retelling of a traditional Jewish story

6

Small beginnings

There was once a young man with big dreams. He lived in a little cottage on the hillside, but in his dreams he imagined living in a beautiful forest, where he would raise a lovely family.

One night as he slept, an angel hovered over him and watched him dreaming of the great oak forest where he would like to live. The next morning he awoke to find a perfect acorn, placed at the foot of his bed.

The next night the angel hovered again and watched him dreaming of a fine flock of swans gliding on the lake in his dream forest. The next morning he awoke to find a small but perfect egg, placed at the foot of his bed.

The third night, as the angel hovered, the young man dreamed of the happy family he would like to raise. The next morning, just as he was waking, he heard a whisper in his ear. It sounded like music, and the music expressed the whisper of an angel – a simple word of love.

Great dreams have small beginnings. A single acorn contains the potential for a whole forest of oak trees. A single egg contains the potential for a whole flock of birds. A single word of love contains the possibility of an entire dynasty of happiness.

Margaret Silf

Free flow

Once there lived a village of creatures along the bottom of a great crystal river. The current of the river swept silently over them all – young and old, rich and poor, good and evil – the current going its own way, knowing only its own crystal self.

Each creature in its own manner clung tightly to the twigs and rocks of the river bottom, for clinging was their way of life, and resisting the current what each had learned from birth.

But one creature said at last, "I am tired of clinging. Though I cannot see it with my eyes, I trust that the current knows where it is going. I shall let go, and let it take me where it will. Clinging, I shall die of boredom."

The other creatures laughed and said, "Fool! Let go, and that current you worship will throw you, tumbled and smashed, across the rocks, and you will die more quickly than from boredom!"

But the one heeded them not, and, taking a breath, did let go, and at once was tumbled and smashed by the current across the rocks.

Yet in time, as the creature refused to cling again, the current lifted him free of the bottom, and he was bruised and hurt no more.

And the creatures downstream, to whom he was a stranger, cried, "See, a miracle! A creature like ourselves, yet he flies! See the Messiah, come to save us all!"

And the one carried in the current said, "I am no more Messiah than you. The river delights to lift us free, if only we dare let go. Our true work is this voyage, this adventure."

But they cried the more, "Saviour!", all the while clinging to the rocks, and when they looked again he was gone, and they were left alone making legends of a saviour.

Richard Bach

Beyond heaven and hell

An angel once walked along the streets of a town. In one hand she carried a torch, and in the other hand she carried a bucket of water.

A surprised passer-by stopped and asked her, "What are you going to do with that fire and that water?"

The angel replied, "With the fire I am going to burn down the mansions of heaven, and with the water I am going to put out the fires of hell. Then we will see who really loves God."

Retelling of a story by Brian Cavanaugh

The gifts department

It was stocktaking time in heaven. The angels were tidying up the gifts department. There was a lot to do. First there was a whole pile of gifts that the Great Giver had offered to the human children, but which had been returned unopened after the recipient's death.

"What a shame," the angels said. "And after the Great Giver chose them so carefully and personally and packaged each one with love."

A second pile then caught their attention – gifts that had been sent back with requests for exchange, and notes attached, such as "This doesn't fit me", or "I'll never be able to use this", or "Please could I exchange this gift for the gift you sent my friend?"

"What a shame," the angels said. "As if the Great Giver doesn't know exactly which gift is right for which person."

And just as they were sighing over all this waste, the Great Giver himself walked into the room. He smiled ruefully as he noticed the piles of unused and unwanted gifts but then broke into a peal of joyous laughter as he reached a special corner of the gifts department where there was *nothing* at all.

"Put some lovely flowers here," he said to the angels, "and prepare a feast. We will have a celebration. This is where the gifts once were that have been sent out, received, welcomed, and completely used up and spent. What joy it is in heaven to see this empty shelf."

Margaret Silf

10

The gardener and the heart surgeon

A gardener once worked for a heart surgeon. The heart surgeon was an atheist. The gardener was a man of faith. They got on very well together, but often had friendly arguments about the nature of life, and faith, and the spiritual life.

One day the heart surgeon thought he had finally settled the argument when he told the gardener: "You talk about 'soul', but let me tell you that I have cut open thousands of human hearts in the course of my career, but not once have I found a 'soul' inside."

"Well," replied the gardener, "I have to tell you that in the course of my work over all these long years in your garden, I have accidentally sliced through many buried daffodil bulbs with my spade, but I have never seen a daffodil inside them."

Source unknown

Guilty as charged

"Prisoner at the bar," said the Grand Inquisitor, "you are charged with encouraging people to break the laws, traditions, and customs of our holy religion. How do you plead?"

"Guilty, your honour."

"And with frequenting the company of heretics, prostitutes, public sinners, the extortionist tax-collectors, the colonial conquerors of our nation – in short, the excommunicated. How do you plead?"

"Guilty, your honour."

"Also with publicly criticizing and denouncing those who have been placed in authority within the church. How do you plead?"

"Guilty, your honour."

"Finally, you are charged with revising, correcting, calling into question the sacred tenets of our faith. How do you plead?"

"Guilty, your honour."

"What is your name, prisoner?"

"Jesus Christ, your honour."

Anthony de Mello

The king's feast

There was once a very kind and noble king. He loved his people so much that he would have given his life for any one of them. And his people loved him dearly in return and they were so happy that they lived in his kingdom.

One day the kind king announced that he was going to hold a great feast, and everyone in the kingdom was invited. He began to make the preparations for the feast. He arranged for fine food and wine to be delivered. He ordered tables and chairs enough for every man, woman, and child in his kingdom. He issued a proclamation inviting all to come to the feast.

As the time for the feast drew closer, the king had to journey to a neighbouring land on royal business. He called his servants together and gave them instructions to complete the preparations in his absence, and promised that he would do his best to return in time for the feast.

The servants duly prepared the tables, and arranged the final details.

On the day of the feast the king returned, delighted to be with his people again and to share the feast with them. But his joy was short-lived. There were many empty places at the feast. And there were many in the kingdom who stood at a distance, too fearful to come to the table.

And he was appalled to learn that in his absence his servants had taken it upon themselves to decide who would be allowed to attend the feast and who would not.

And so it came to pass that before the feast could begin, the king personally called in all those whom the servants had rejected, and gave them the places of honour. And the wicked servants? Well, they were required to serve everyone else with food and drink before they were allowed to take their own place at the bottom table.

Margaret Silf

The new Jesus

It happened in Papua New Guinea in the 1980s. Many of the traditional huts of the people had been replaced by European-style buildings. The church too was European in style, with a European crucifix on the altar.

Then one day something terrible happened. The termites ate Jesus, and he fell off the cross, splitting into splinters of wood.

A local sculptor called Ketson was invited to carve a new Jesus in native style, but when he had finished his carving, he couldn't bring himself to nail the new Jesus to the cross. He asked other friends around the village, but none of them could bring themselves to put the nails into Jesus.

Eventually they had a different idea. "We will not nail Jesus back on the cross," they decided. "We will suspend the new Jesus *above* the cross, and from now on he will speak to us every day of his rising."

Margaret Silf

14

Why pray?

A disciple once asked his master, "What can I do to attain God?"

The master answered by asking the disciple another question: "What can you do to make the sun rise?"

The disciple retorted indignantly, "Nothing at all. So why are you giving us all these methods of prayer?"

And the master replied, "To make sure you're awake when the sun rises."

Source unknown

Knowing
Ourselves

15

Chickens can't fly

Once upon a time a female eagle, on a long and lonely flight, became weary and needed to stop for a rest. As she came down to land, she caught sight of a sheltered spot, and made a nest for herself to rest in for a while. While she was there the time came for her to lay an egg, so she stayed even longer, to guard her egg and keep it warm.

But just before the egg was due to hatch, there was a great disruption. A farmer came along and started to erect fencing all around her. Of course, being an eagle, she was easily able to fly free of the fencing and soar to the skies. But she had to leave her egg behind.

The next day the farmer's work was completed, and the area had become a brand-new chicken run. The farmer installed a dozen chickens in their new home, just as the eagle chick was hatching. No one noticed that there were now thirteen birds in the chicken run.

And so it happened that the eagle chick grew up among the chickens. It was a comfortable life. Food arrived regularly, and the chicken run was kept warm and dry, and safe from predators. What more could a baby eagle ask for?

Time passed, and the eagle grew. One day a travelling ornithologist passed by, noticed the eagle, and stopped to talk.

"Don't you know you are an eagle?" he asked.

"Don't be silly," said the eagle. "I'm a chicken. I live in a chicken run. I eat with the chickens. I behave like a chicken. How would I not be a chicken? Anyway," he added, "I can't fly. Chickens don't fly."

"But you *can* fly," the ornithologist assured him. "You just haven't tried."

"Why would I fly anywhere?" asked the eagle. "I have everything I could wish for here in the chicken run."

"Everything except freedom," the ornithologist replied. "The freedom to be who you are destined to be."

"I don't have any destiny beyond the chicken run," the eagle said.

"So you are happy to end up on someone's dinner plate when you could be soaring to the skies?"

"I will do what chickens do," the eagle insisted. "I *am* a chicken."

And so the ornithologist gave up and went on his way. Some time later, however, there was another passing visitor to the chicken run. One day there was a sweep and a whoosh, and a majestic golden eagle winged his way across the heavens. Perhaps he called silently as he flew, called to the eagle chick down in the chicken run, called with the cry that only the heart can hear. Something fluttered inside the eagle chick, and his feathers quivered, and his wings flapped, opened, and carried him, falteringly, to the top of the chicken-run fence.

"What are you doing?" the chickens asked him. "Get down, before you fall. Chickens can't fly."

But their warnings came too late. The eagle chick had responded to the call of the skies. He was already soaring beyond their vision, following the trail of his ancient destiny.

Retelling of a traditional story

16

Crisis among the bees

There was once a forest of trees, each living a full life in its own way. But, in the natural order of things, over time each tree grew old and eventually died.

Meanwhile, various groups of bees had made their nests in the hollow tree trunks, where they lived happily, and produced their honey, and the honey of each different group of bees was subtly different in flavour from that of the other groups.

Then, one by one, the trees began to die and fall.

The bees debated the meaning of this and decided it must be a reflection of the merits of the bees who lived in each tree. Some believed that if a tree fell, the bees in that tree were being punished for a failure in true belief. Others, feeling compassion, tried to help the bees who had become homeless by sharing their own nests. Others pronounced that the homeless bees had clearly been flawed from the very beginning and were predestined to lose their tree and die.

But, finally, all the trees died, and all the bees were homeless. Each group was shocked. All had thought that the trees were about the bees, and failed to see the wider reality of the forest or respect its nature. All had believed that their group was the one true hive, destined to be saved and to establish a new age. None had realized that they all lived in the uncertainty and precariousness of a changing, evolving world, and that each was called to complete its own particular task and then move on to another forest. None had looked beyond its own life or been able to see itself as part of a greater wholeness.

Retelling of a Sufi story

Hearts and voices

There was once a young girl of twelve years old, who had a beautiful voice. Her parents were wondering whether they should send her to music school to have her voice professionally trained, but they hesitated, not sure whether she would pass an audition and not wanting to expose her to unnecessary stress and the risk of rejection.

So they invited a family friend, a celebrated musician, to come along one evening and listen to their daughter informally. And so the girl sang for him. When she had finished there was a long silence, while she and her parents anxiously awaited his verdict.

Finally he broke the silence. "She sings beautifully," he said. "When her heart has been broken she will sing sublimely."

Source unknown

Ice sculpture

A Norwegian artist loved to make ice sculptures. When winter came he would travel to the Arctic north and camp in a shack beside the frozen river. He would hack slabs of ice from the river and carve them into beautiful shapes.

People soon heard about his work and came from far and wide to see these sculptures.

"Doesn't it sadden you", they asked, "that, as soon as the spring thaw begins, your art will vanish back into the river?"

"Not at all," he replied, "for this is our life. For a brief time we take material form, and have a unique opportunity to express something of the nature of the spirit within us. If we express that spirit truthfully and honestly, others will find inspiration from it. And then, when the time is right, we return peacefully to the river, and all is well."

Margaret Silf

Is this who I am?

Once upon a time a man was walking along the lakeside on a bright, calm, sunny day. He stopped to gaze at the lake, and saw in the still water his own reflection, and was fascinated by what he saw.

"Is this who I am?" he pondered to himself.

The next day, wanting to remind himself of this marvel, he returned to the lakeside. But overnight the weather had changed. A strong wind now ruffled the water, and his image now seemed to him to be distracted and disturbed.

"Is this who I really am?" he wondered.

The next day he went again to the lakeshore, but now the bad weather had set in and it was raining. His reflection in the lake was blurred and indistinct. It seemed to him that it was a very confused version of himself that stared back at him from the water.

Time passed, and one day an enormous storm blew up. Eager to see the lake in this weather, the man went to the shore again, and this time the self he saw reflected there was full of anger, raging at the dark skies overhead.

"Is this the real me?" he asked himself.

And all the while the sly fox Iktomi had been watching the man's reactions.

The man heard a low growl of mirth in the bushes, and turned to see the fox laughing at him.

"You foolish human," said the fox. "You are looking at what is merely a reflection of who you are, changing with every passing mood of the weather. How can you believe that this is the real you?"

"But where *is* the real me?" enquired the man.

"Come back here in the depths of winter and you will find who you are," said the fox.

And so it came to pass that winter arrived, and the lake froze solid, and snow fell, covering everything that grew on the lakeside. The man returned, and gazed at the pristine whiteness of the silent lake.

"There is no 'me' in the lake any more," he said to the fox sitting patiently beside him.

"Exactly so," said the fox. "Now you can no longer settle for these passing images or projections of yourself. The lake is an empty canvas. It invites you to become the person you truly are. Look inside your own heart. Look deeper than your passing moods. There you will discover who you are."

Retelling of a traditional Lakota story

Rich man, poor man?

There was once a wealthy city executive who wanted his son to understand that not everyone in the world was as fortunate. So he took the boy on a trip to a poor part of the country, and stayed for a day and a night with a family that was trying to scratch a living from the land.

When they got back home, the father asked the boy how he felt about the experience.

"It was amazing, Dad," the boy replied.

"So you saw how hard it can be for some people just to stay alive?"

"Yes," the boy agreed.

"And what did you learn?"

The boy thought carefully before making his reply. Then…

"I noticed that we have a dog at home who is well groomed and pampered, and they have four dogs who run free. We have an artificial pool in our garden; they have a stream that flows right through their land. We have electric lights on our deck; they have the stars. We have a small front garden with a fence; they have an endless horizon. We have smart phones and a TV in every room; they have conversations around the table. We have stress; they have time."

The father was speechless, but the son continued, "Thanks, Dad, for showing me that wealth is not always what you think it is, and that there are riches that money can't buy."

Retelling of a story by Brian Campbell SJ

Running mates

Only the very best Qualities had been selected to compete in the human Olympics. The track events were arousing a great deal of interest. The two favourites were Enthusiasm and Commitment. But who would win the gold?

In the short sprints, Enthusiasm was coming through with flying colours. But the big test was the marathon. Enthusiasm took off at a great speed, and far outstripped all the other runners. Commitment was way back. It looked like a done deal. But, halfway through the race, Enthusiasm started to flag. Would she even make it to the finishing post? Commitment was closing in… Commitment was overtaking on the last leg of the circuit. Commitment was home!

When the excitement died down, the two running mates shook hands.

"You always get things going," said Commitment to Enthusiasm. "I really admire your energy."

"But I never make the distance on my own," admitted Enthusiasm. "It's you who bring things to completion."

And from then on, they always ran together, never seeing each other as competitors, but as collaborators in the race of life.

Margaret Silf

The bedtime story

Teffie was a bright and happy three-year-old, with a vivid imagination. She loved to chatter all day long, and when bedtime came she loved to hear the bedtime stories her mother used to read. Secretly Teffie wanted to write stories herself, but she still didn't go to school, and didn't know how to write.

Teffie's mum was a very special person who loved her daughter dearly. Imagine her surprise one evening, as she was sitting on the edge of Teffie's bed, the storybook open on her lap, when her little daughter announced that she wanted to write a bedtime story herself tonight.

And so Teffie's mum reached along the shelf for a writing pad and pencil and gave it to her daughter. For five minutes Teffie scribbled eagerly in the pad, filling page after page.

"Have you finished your story?" asked Mum.

"Yes," said Teffie with a satisfied smile. "Now will you read it to me, please, Mum?"

Slightly taken aback by this request, Mum nevertheless took the pad, and carefully perused the scribbles. And then, as if the text were right there in front of her, she told a brand-new story of how Teffie had rescued a kitten from a tall tree, and the kitten had then turned into a beautiful fairy and given Teffie three wishes. The story went on for ten minutes and Teffie was entranced.

When Mum had finished, Teffie said, "Mum, did I really write that story?"

"Well," said Mum, "you didn't put the words on the paper exactly, but the story was right there inside you. I just helped you to get it out."

And Teffie smiled a deep contented smile as she turned over and fell asleep.

Story generously shared from the personal experience of Mary Robertson

The hidden princess

Once upon a time, in a valley deep in the Canadian Rockies, there lived a beautiful queen called Queen Louise. She was so beautiful, in her vivid blue robe shimmering under the azure skies, that her neighbour, the great glacier Wenkchemna, fell in love with her and by and by they had a daughter, whom they named Princess Moraine.

Now it came to pass that as the little princess grew into a beautiful young woman, her mother began to feel jealous of her. Many people came to visit Queen Louise and admire her outstanding beauty, but the queen noticed that even more people were coming to admire her lovely daughter. So one day she decided to banish the little princess by sending her high up into a remote valley that could be reached only by a long, winding, climbing trail, which only the most determined of visitors would undertake. Yet still the visitors came in search of the beautiful, elusive princess. So the queen sought the advice of the ten great mountains who stood guard over the valley.

"Never fear, your majesty," the mountains rumbled. "We will arrange to send avalanches down the valley every winter, so that no one will be able to enter the hiding place of the princess. And so it came to be that for eight months of every year Princess Moraine was all alone in her remote resting place, and no one could reach her or gaze upon her beauty.

The princess was sad and lonely as she lay there in her valley. She gazed up at her father, the mighty glacier, who looked down with love upon her, and saw her sorrow.

"Fear not, my dear daughter," he said. "I will send ice and snow to cover you through the winter, and keep you safe from harm. And when the summer returns, your beauty will be greater than ever."

And so it was. Gradually the queen began to regret her impetuous action in sending her daughter so far up the remote valley. Her earlier jealousy turned to pride in her beautiful daughter. She began to whisper to the many people who visited her: "Go a little further. Go where it is not so easy. Let your footsteps lead you to the deeper reaches of your heart. And there you will find a jewel of great price, hidden among ten mountain peaks."

And so, during the four months of the year when the avalanches receded and the sun shone bright, those who had heard the whispers of the queen did go further, did risk the road less travelled, and did discover a jewel beyond price – a sapphire sparkling among the peaks.

And in the quiet of the starlit nights, the great glacier Wenkchemna would bend low over his daughter and kiss her brow and whisper his ancient wisdom: "When we venture deeper behind the face we present to the world, and risk visiting those parts of ourselves that we try to hide, we discover an inner beauty that only a few will see. Those who come to your shores, Princess Moraine, will look upon your beauty, and see their own heart's treasure reflected back to them. And when they see the hidden beauty in themselves, from that moment on they will always see the inner beauty in others. And they will be counted among the blessed, for they will return to their homes having tasted joy, and that joy shall never be taken from them."

Margaret Silf

The seal woman

One evening a man was taking a walk along the shore and came upon a group of beautiful girls, dancing gracefully in the moonlight. Beside them lay what looked like furs.

The man's approach startled them, and they all reached for their skins, put them on and plunged into the sea, and then the man could see that in truth they were seals.

One seal, however, was too slow. The man had picked up her skin and she couldn't dive back into the water without it, so the man took her by the hand and led her back to his home to be his wife.

In this new life, she was very unhappy and missed her home in the sea very much. Time passed and they had three children, but always deep in her heart she longed to be a seal again.

One evening when their father was out, the children were playing. In their game they dislodged an old box from the top of a cupboard. After they had gone to bed, when their mother was tidying up the toys, she found this dusty old box and opened it up, and what should she discover inside it but – to her great joy – her old skin.

That night she crept into her children's rooms and bade them all farewell, went silently down to the shore by moonlight and returned to being who she truly was.

This could be a sad story, but it has a happy ending, for, every night, those three children can be seen in the bay conversing with a beautiful seal, who, every night, gives them counsel and blessing, even as she bestows a blessing upon all who live in the bay.

When we are true to who we really are, we are the blessing we are created to be.

Source unknown

The talking teacup

Two grandparents were looking for a special gift for their little granddaughter on her birthday.

Eventually they found the perfect gift – a beautiful teacup. Granddad held it up to examine it carefully, and declared, "What a truly beautiful teacup, the loveliest I have ever seen. Let's buy it for her."

Imagine his surprise, then, when the teacup began to talk. And right there in the shop, she told her story…

"Thank you for your kind comments," she said, "but I wasn't always beautiful. Once upon a time I was an ugly, soggy lump of clay. Then a man with dirty wet hands picked me up and threw me onto a big wheel. The wheel was turning, turning, making me feel dizzy, and I begged him to stop. I thought I would die on that wheel. But the man refused to stop. He poked me and punched me until I hurt all over, but still he wouldn't stop.

"And finally he put me into a firing kiln, and I could hardly bear the terrible intense heat.

"When it cooled down at last and I was taken out, another horror awaited me. A lady began to paint me, and I thought the dreadful fumes from the paint would suffocate me, but she wouldn't stop. And when she finished, she put me right back in the kiln again.

"But at long last the world became cool once more. I was placed on a shelf, beside a mirror. I could hardly believe my eyes. There I was – beautiful, fine, clean – and useful!

"I cried for joy, that something so beautiful could emerge out of all that pain.

"So when you give me to your little granddaughter, please don't forget to tell her my story. Who knows? The time may come when she will need my story as much as she needs *me*."

Retelling of a story by William J. Bausch

The man and the mask

Oliver was a man of many parts – a well-known actor, a household name. Millions of people had seen him on stage and on screen. They thought they "knew" him. But Oliver was a man behind a mask. Every night when he got home to his apartment the first thing he did was take off his mask. Only then could he relax and be himself.

As time passed, however, he began to notice some strange and unpleasant effects. Each night as he stripped off the mask it felt a bit more sticky. It hurt his skin as he pulled himself free of it. And then, one night, he couldn't get the mask off at all. It had welded itself right into his skin. It had become permanent.

Of course, his acting career went from strength to strength. But when he got home and looked in the mirror, a desperate voice inside him seemed to cry out reproachfully: "Who are you really? You have set solid in a role that isn't you. You have become a person you are not."

Oliver felt utterly empty. His many fans would never have guessed, for he played his many roles unerringly, but inside was a hollow, nameless space where his true self had once lived. And so it continued for many long and empty years.

But the angels were not idle. One night an old friend came by. They hadn't met in years. She took a long, deep look at him, the joy of reunion glowing in her eyes.

"Oliver," she murmured. "How very good to see you again."

And at that moment Oliver knew once more who he really was. It had needed just one person, one true friend, one loving heart to see the man beneath the mask. And gradually, painlessly, the mask loosened and slipped away.

Margaret Silf

To be a platypus

There was once a duck who lived with all the other ducks in a sheltered part of the river. But she was an adventurous duck, and one day she swam off on her own further down the river to see what lay beyond her limited horizon.

Eventually she grew tired and stopped to rest on the riverbank. What she did not realize, however, was that she was resting on the top of the nest of a water rat. The water rat, delighted to find this sitting duck on top of his nest, seized her and took her down into his nest, where she was forced to become his wife.

But one day, several weeks later, the water rat fell asleep in the afternoon sun on the riverbank. The duck took her opportunity, slipped into the river, and swam rapidly back to the other ducks, who were, of course, very pleased to see her.

The time came for the ducks to lay their eggs and they were all very happy. Then the time came for the eggs to hatch, and they were all happy to have their ducklings. But our adventurous duck was shocked when the little creature that emerged from her egg was a strange mixture of bird and rat. The other ducks were likewise shocked at this aberration, and they drove her off and would have nothing more to do with her. And this was how the platypus was created. Our story now switches to aboriginal dreamtime, the beginning of creation.

All the creatures were trying to decide who belonged to which tribe. When they came to the platypus, they all wanted him to be in their tribe.

The tribe of the birds said, "You are clearly a bird. You have a beak and you lay eggs. Welcome to the tribe of the birds."

The platypus answered politely, "Thank you for your kind

invitation. I'll think about it."

The tribe of the mammals said, "You are clearly a mammal, for you have fur and you suckle your young. Welcome to the tribe of the mammals."

The platypus answered politely, "Thank you for your kind invitation. I'll think about it."

The tribe of the fish said, "You are clearly a fish. See how wonderfully you dart through the water. Welcome to the tribe of the fish."

The platypus answered politely, "Thank you for your kind invitation. I'll think about it."

And after a while the platypus returned to the great gathering of the tribes, and said this: "I thank you most sincerely for your kindness and your welcome. It's true, I do feel a strong affinity with each of your tribes and I am proud to be connected with you. But actually, I'm a platypus. And it's OK just to be a platypus!"

Retelling of an Australian aboriginal story

Unplanned gift

A princess once lived in the noisiest kingdom in the whole world. The king and queen loved their daughter dearly, and when her fourteenth birthday came around they wanted to give her a special surprise. They thought long and hard about this, and then they came up with an idea. "Let's arrange to give her the very loudest birthday cheer that the world has ever known," they decided.

And so they sent messages all across the land. At noon precisely on the princess's birthday, they asked everyone in the kingdom to give the loudest cheer they were capable of. All together they would raise such a cheer as never was heard before.

Everyone was very excited about this. They all agreed to take part, but secretly they all had a rather different thought. "No one will miss *my* voice among so many," they thought to themselves. "I will just keep quiet and listen, because it would be so amazing to hear the loudest cheer in the whole world."

The day of the princess's birthday arrived. The clock advanced towards noon. Everyone was holding their breath. The king and queen had brought their daughter to the castle door to receive her special gift, but she had no idea what it might be. She was really excited about the great surprise that awaited her.

Finally, the clock struck twelve. And what happened? Total and complete silence! Everyone had been wanting to hear the great cheer, and everyone was silently listening for it, thinking that their voice would not be missed among so many.

The king and queen were shocked that their great surprise could have gone so wrong. For five whole minutes everyone remained silent, not knowing rightly what to say.

And the princess? She stood there at the castle door, her eyes alight with pure joy, listening intently. Eventually she turned to embrace her parents. "Thank you so much for this wonderful birthday gift," she said. "I never imagined there could be something so wonderful in the world. What a beautiful surprise." Her parents looked amazed at her reaction. She went on, "I have lived in this kingdom for fourteen whole years now, and there has always been noise everywhere. I thought that was how the world is. But today I have discovered something new and wonderful. Absolute quiet. I never knew that birds could sing. I never heard the wind in the trees. I never heard the little creatures scuttling through the undergrowth. I never heard my own heart beating. I never knew that it is possible to hear God speak. I will always cherish this gift of silence you have given me today. I will carry it constantly in my heart, and I will keep on taking it out to wrap around me, whenever the noise is overwhelming."

Source unknown

Hurting and Healing

Bread for the enemy

It was a bleak day in the bleak year of 1944 in Moscow. Some 20,000 German prisoners-of-war were being marched across Red Square. The mood was grim and angry. Most people present had had a husband, a brother, a son, a father, a lover killed in the conflict. The police were having trouble holding them back behind the cordons. Some spectators were ready to tear the now-vanquished enemy limb from limb.

The captured officers led the parade. Heads still held high, in an attitude perceived by the crowd as arrogance, they were jeered and spat upon as they passed. And then came the ordinary soldiers – a very different picture. Men on crutches, barely able to hobble across the Square; men wrapped in blood-soaked bandages; men whose eyes were pools of terror; men wracked by exhaustion, starvation, and abject humiliation.

Silence fell over Red Square. The people who had suffered so much at the hands of this enemy now looked into the eyes and faces of thousands of fellow human beings teetering on the very edge of desperation.

And then one woman broke through the cordon. In her hand she held a piece of black bread from her own kitchen, bread she could ill afford to give away. Before anyone could stop her she thrust it into the hand of a German prisoner. Others saw her gesture. Others also had bread in their homes. Others also recognized the human being behind the enemy uniform and broke through the cordons to give what bread they could. Soon the scene of triumphalist scorn turned to one of human compassion. A bleak moment in human history became a moment of transformation.

Retelling of a true story by Yevgeny Yevtushenko

Christmas lights

The whole country was in deep recession.

Nearly half of the people in one small town had no work. There was an atmosphere of dejection and hopelessness everywhere. Christmas was approaching, but there was very little money to buy gifts or festive food. And then came the final straw. When the townsfolk started to assemble the traditional Christmas lights to decorate the streets, they found that the lights were no longer working.

At first everyone turned to the mayor. "Our Christmas lights are faulty. What are you going to do about it?"

And the mayor summoned the town council for a meeting. "The Christmas lights have failed. What can we do about it?" he asked.

"There is no money available to buy new Christmas lights," they told him. "We are barely surviving. There is nothing left over for luxuries like that."

And the mayor told the people the bad news, and at first the people were angry. They wanted to complain to the mayor and protest to the town council. But eventually they too could see that there was simply no money, and that was the end of the matter.

And then the Christmas miracle began. A few of the townsfolk got together. "I am an electrician," said one. "Maybe I can fix the lights."

"And I have an axe and a saw," said another. "I could fetch a big fir tree from the forest to place in the town square."

"And I have a long ladder," said another. "I can help put the lights on the tree."

"I'm no good with technical things," said another, "but I can bake. I will make mince pies for everyone."

"Oh," another spoke up. "In that case, I can make hot chocolate for all the children on Christmas Eve."

"And I will make mulled wine for the grown-ups," offered the innkeeper.

And so it happened that the town celebrated Christmas that year in such a special way that no one who was there would ever, ever forget it.

Margaret Silf

Moving the fence

In the Australian outback there lived a tribe of aboriginal people who had carried out their sacred rituals and ceremonies since time immemorial.

One day a missionary arrived from Europe. The tribespeople made him welcome and he was eager to learn from them about their sacred pathways, just as they were willing to learn from him about the story of his God.

They listened to his teaching, and some of them began to attend mass every day, and some of them never attended mass, and some of them attended when they felt like it. But they all lived contentedly in community.

Then after many years the first missionary died and a new one was sent. He had a very different attitude. He gathered them all together on his first day and told them they must all attend mass, otherwise they would go to hell, and they must immediately stop all their "pagan" practices.

And so some of them attended mass every day, and some of them never attended, and some of them attended when they felt like it. In short, nothing changed.

Until the tribal chief died.

Now the tribal chief never attended mass, but his wife attended daily. Imagine the consternation of his wife, therefore, when the missionary priest announced that the tribal chief could not be buried in consecrated ground.

The elders consulted with all the people of the tribe, and it was decided to comply with the missionary priest's dictate. That the tribal chief must be buried with all the ancient ceremonies was clear.

That this could not happen in the churchyard was also clear. And therefore the people of the tribe carried out their funeral ceremonies just outside the fence that bordered the churchyard, while the priest looked on, powerless to intervene.

Night fell, and the chief had been duly buried with full tribal honours.

And in the night, six of the strongest young men of the tribe came along and *moved the fence*.

And so it came to be that the chief departed to his eternal rest from consecrated ground.

Margaret Silf

Learning to forget

Hundreds of years ago there had been a bitter battle between two tribes who lived in the same country. No one could actually remember what the battle had been about, but everyone remembered that it had happened, and to this day people descended from those two tribes were still antagonistic towards each other, so entrenched was the bitter memory.

One of these distant descendants was a teacher at the local primary school. One day he was supervising the children as they stood in line to see Santa at their annual Christmas party. Imagine his shock when one child suddenly turned round and, unprovoked, hit out at the child standing behind him.

"Stop that!" he said, calling the young offender out of the line. "Why did you hit your schoolmate?"

"He started it," said the boy.

"No, he didn't," the teacher replied. "I was watching you standing in line. I saw it all. You can't tell me that he started it."

"Yes, he did," protested the boy. "He hit me first."

"When did he hit you?" asked the teacher.

"Last Easter," said the boy.

And that night the teacher decided it was time to make a phone call to one of his neighbours who was descended from the other tribe, and finally start the work of letting go of old resentments.

Margaret Silf

The mandolin man

In a kingdom long ago the king was gravely ill. Now he was a wise and gentle king, and everyone cared about him and wished him well, but no one knew what to do to cure his sickness.

One day a stranger came by, carrying a mandolin. He played his music in the streets, but he sensed immediately that there was sorrow in the town. His mandolin quivered and trembled and would play only sad songs.

"Why is no one smiling in this land?" he asked, eventually. And then the people told him about the king's grievous illness.

"Perhaps I can help," he suggested. "Perhaps my mandolin has some wisdom to offer you." And he began to play. And the song he sang told of a sick man's search for healing and for joy. The crowd listened intently, wondering how this song might help the king. When the mandolin man got to the final stanza, they received their answer. "*The king needs to wear the shirt of a happy man,*" the song finished with a flourish.

Now that the people knew the remedy, they began to search. They searched among the nobility, but the noblemen were all concerned about increasing their wealth and cultivating their ambitions. They searched among the merchants, but the merchants were all struggling with their worries about the recession and rising costs. They searched among the peasants, but the peasants were all feeling resentful and oppressed and planning a revolt.

There was deep gloom all over the land. Then one day the search party heard the sound of singing in the forest. As they drew nearer they saw a poor man sitting there, enjoying a simple meal, and so happy to have the sunlight on his back and the trees above him, a bit of bread and cheese to eat and fresh spring water to drink. Here, at last, was a happy man. They would take his shirt.

But there lay the next problem. The poor but happy man *had* no shirt.

The singing continued. The peace and contentment of the place, and the man, began to sink into the searchers. And when the moment was right the mandolin appeared among the trees, playing the tune the poor man was singing.

"*Learn from me,*" the words rang out, "*and you can all be as happy as I am. Let your troubles sink and your hearts rise. Learn from me.*"

The mandolin man left the city soon after that, but his melody lingered on. Soon the king was offered more shirts than he could possibly wear, and the clouds lifted from the city of sorrows.

Retelling of a traditional story

The people who were always hungry

There was once a kingdom way beyond the ocean, where all the people were contented and the king was kind and generous.

But, as time went on, voyagers came from far away bringing new kinds of food and drink to sell to the people of the happy kingdom. The king tried every new type of food that was brought, and he ate more and more, and became more and more rotund. He spread the word among the people that there are all kinds of good things to eat in the wider world, and encouraged them also to eat and eat, until they were almost too full to move.

And it was then that they began to notice something very strange. After they had eaten their fill of every feast imaginable, they felt strangely uncomfortable. At first they tried to ignore these feelings of discomfort. They tried to suppress the feelings of dissatisfaction gnawing away inside them.

But children often speak the truth that adults deny. "I'm hungry!" a child spoke up eventually.

"Don't be silly," the adults replied. "You can't be hungry. You have just eaten a whole feast."

But the child persisted, in the way of little children: "I'm hungry!"

And when they stopped to think about it, those who were honest with themselves had to admit the unspeakable truth: "We are hungry." And gradually it became clear, at least to those among the people who walked with open eyes through the world: "The more we eat, the more hungry we feel."

Yet there seemed to be no way out of this vicious circle. The more they had, the more they wanted, the more they consumed, and the hungrier they felt. The voyagers had put some evil spell on them, they believed. But who could break the spell?

For a long time nothing changed. And when change came it was, once more, a little child who opened up the door to freedom. She was only five years old, and all her short life she had loved to roam along the seashore, smell the flowers on the mountainside, play with the wild creatures and watch the clouds scudding past in the sky. She had learned to love the touch of the sun on her skin in summer, and the crunch of the crisp new snow in winter. She had watched the first shy flower emerge from the ground in spring, and played "catch" with falling leaves in autumn.

Her godmother noticed all this, and one day she asked the little girl, "Don't you ever get hungry, like the rest of us?"

At first the little girl didn't understand the question. She always enjoyed a modest share of any feast that was going, but she always stopped before she got too full, so that she could go out to play.

"Why would I feel hungry?" she asked her godmother, puzzled. "Every day there is a new feast for me to enjoy. Come out with me. I'll show you."

And so a change began. Gradually, guided by the children, one after another of the people of the kingdom started to enjoy the treasures around them that would never run out. They no longer needed the rich food that the voyagers brought, which would go off if they didn't eat it all quickly. Even the king began to suffer less and less from the cravings of hunger for the things that wouldn't last. And as time passed, the kingdom became, once again, a place of joy and contentment.

Margaret Silf

The prince's statue

There was once a handsome prince, but he had a crooked back. This always seemed to hold him back from realizing his full potential in life. He had a very negative image of himself and always expected others to be critical or patronizing, and, even when people praised him, he could never quite believe that their admiration was genuine.

One day his father, the king, called the best sculptor in the land and asked him to carve a statue of the prince. This was duly done. The sculptor, who admired the prince very much, created a beautiful statue of him, but carved the figure of the prince with a straight back.

The finished statue was placed in the central courtyard of the royal palace, where the prince saw it every day as he went about his business.

And gradually, over the months and years that followed, a miracle happened. Whenever he passed by the statue and stopped to gaze up at it, he seemed to hear a voice inside inviting him to reach up to everything he could be. And so it happened that his back grew more and more straight, and he walked tall, becoming day by day more fully the person the king always knew he really was.

Retelling of a story by Brian Cavanaugh

The quarrelling tools

Once upon a time, a long time ago, in a little village in a far northern country, there was a carpenter's workshop.

One day, when the carpenter was away for a while, a mighty quarrel broke out on the workbench, among the tools. The dispute went on and on, and became more and more embittered. The argument was about the need to exclude certain tools from the community.

"We really have to exclude Sister Saw," one of the tools began. "She bites, and she grinds her teeth. She has the most peevish character anyone could imagine."

"We absolutely can't keep Brother Plane among us any longer," another tool chimed in. "He has a cruel nature, scraping at everything he touches."

"As for Brother Hammer," a third insisted, "I find him such a bore, and rowdy with it. He thumps away all the time and gets on all our nerves. Let's get rid of him."

"And what about the nails?" asked a fourth. "How can we be expected to live alongside such sharp characters? They're a positive hazard to us all. And the file and the rasp as well. Living with them is one constant cause of friction! And, while we're about it, we should send the sandpaper away, because she seems to be the reason why this workshop is in such a fractious mood."

And the whole dispute rapidly became a battleground of all the tools, each one trying to out-shout the others. History doesn't record whether it was the hammer who accused the saw, or the plane who objected to the nails, but the outcome of the melee was that *all* the tools found themselves excluded!

The fracas came to a sudden end, however, on the return of the carpenter to his workshop. All the tools fell silent when they saw him approaching.

He picked up a plank of wood, and cut it with the biting Sister Saw. He smoothed it down with cruel, scraping Brother Plane. With boring, rowdy Brother Hammer he drove in the sharp, hazardous nails. Using rough-natured Brother File and abrasive Sister Sandpaper he made a velvet finish on the wood.

Not a single one of the tools was left out as the carpenter went about his task of creating...

...a cradle!

A cradle to receive a little child.

A cradle to receive Life.

Retelling of a Swedish folk story

The ring that refused to go away

The ring's story begins long ago and far away. Or perhaps it was only yesterday, and very close to home. This you must decide for yourself. The story begins, as all good stories should, with love. A prince and a princess, or perhaps a very ordinary girl and boy, were once very much in love. Their lives stretched out before them like a beckoning promise. There was nothing that lay beyond the reach of their hopes and dreams. They exchanged rings as a token of their love. The sun seemed to shine down unstintingly upon their carefree days. Until the black cloud gathered its power against them, rising up from the horizon, darkening their hearts with anger and distrust.

When the storm broke out from the depths of the black cloud they quarrelled. They hurled bitter reproaches at each other like lightning flashes and thunderclaps. The princess walked away, declaring that she never wanted to see her prince again. Winter came, and snow covered the hardened ground, and the ice of unforgiveness froze the place where once love had blossomed. The prince's heart was crumpled. It twisted into the shape of sorrow and stayed that way. In his rage against his lost love, he hurled his ring far away into the deep snows, as if to cast away his pain. But when spring returned and the snows melted, a little boy from the village found it lying on the grass, and brought it back to the prince, for his initials were engraved inside it, alongside those of his lost princess.

Years passed, and the prince, now grown into an angry warlord, took the ring to the jeweller's shop and sold it. Perhaps now, he thought, he would be rid of its unhappy spell. But a few weeks later an old friend of the prince found the ring in a second-hand shop, and, recognizing his friend's initials, redeemed it for its rightful owner. Would nothing break the ring's malignant power, the prince wondered. Would he ever be able to purge the bitter memories?

The prince grew old, a surly, lonely old man, suffering from one undefined illness after another, as though even his body was in a permanent state of anger and reproach. People avoided him and his sullen, silent wrath. He sank into penury.

Desperate for relief for his aching body and soul, he sought out the wise woman who lived in the valley. "You are a very sick man," she told him. "Your body will not recover until your mind and heart are healed."

"I have no money," he told the wise woman, "but I can give you this gold ring instead."

The wise woman took the ring and looked at the initials engraved within it. There, with her wise eyes, she read the story. "My prescription for your ills is this," she told him. "You must wear this ring. It has your name on it." And with this instruction, she sent him on his way.

And so the prince, in his despair, did as the wise woman had told him. He slipped the ring onto his finger for the first time since his one true love had left him. At first it almost burned his finger in two, so painful was its touch. But day by day he gradually began to feel a little better. His bodily anguish lessened. His expression softened. His muscles relaxed. But most importantly of all, his memories lost their angry edge. A gentle wave of forgiveness began to lap at the beaches of his hardened heart. The years of denial were over. The hurting was acknowledged and embraced. The time for healing had arrived.

Margaret Silf

The seafarers' wish

There was once a chaplain who ministered to the needs of seafarers who landed on his shores and were far from home.

One day a container ship docked at the port and the chaplain went out to see whether there was anything that the crew might need. The captain welcomed him warmly as he boarded the boat, and then the chaplain made his offer.

"If there is anything your men might need while they are in port, or if there is somewhere they might like me to take them while they are here, please let me know."

A few hours later the captain came to see him.

"I've asked the crew what they would most like to experience while they are docked here," he told the chaplain.

The chaplain listened attentively, half afraid that the men might have some extravagant wish that he would not be able to fulfil. Then the captain went on: "They asked me to ask you whether you might be able to take them somewhere where they could walk on grass," he said.

And so it happened that the chaplain took these men, mainly Filipino, Ukrainian, and Chinese sailors who had spent the last six months with only heaving steel under their feet, to a nearby park. Once there, they all took off their shoes and socks, and very reverently, and with evident joy, walked barefoot on the fresh grass.

"Anyone would have thought I had given them the earth," he smiled as he told me the story.

"But you *did*," I replied.

Margaret Silf

The Thanksgiving guest

A family in a small American town lived next door to Mrs Casey. The mother of the family used to visit Mrs Casey frequently, bringing her meals and company. This was very much appreciated, because Mrs Casey was actually dying slowly and painfully of a wasting disease that was making her flesh rot. As a result she could never rid herself of an unpleasant smell and was not easy to be near.

Thanksgiving came round, and her kind neighbour invited Mrs Casey to share in the family's Thanksgiving dinner. But there were protests from the two children. The younger boy, especially, told his mother that the smell of Mrs Casey at the table would completely spoil his enjoyment of the dinner, and he refused to sit anywhere near her.

However, when dinner was ready, he found himself seated exactly opposite this poor neighbour. He screwed up his nose and tried to get on with his dinner, eyes lowered, speaking as little as possible, with minimal courtesy, but cold and distant.

The sweet potatoes were passed round – the young boy's favourite. There was enough for one potato for each person, and everyone knew that. But when the dish reached the older brother, he broke the unwritten rule and took two. Mrs Casey must have noticed too, because when the dish reached her, she passed it straight on without taking any. Eventually the dish arrived at the younger brother's place. There was just one sweet potato left in the dish. He looked at it, thought for a moment, and then cut it carefully in two and gave half to Mrs Casey, with a shy, embarrassed smile.

And it was then that something quite amazing happened. He noticed that Mrs Casey didn't seem to smell bad any more! She took the half potato, thanking him with a gracious smile, and they had a wonderful dinner – a genuine Thanksgiving.

Retelling of a story by Sr Jose Hobday

The tin box

The auction sale had been heartbreaking. Bob and Pauline had been married for forty years, during which time they had been through many struggles, and had finally divorced. Unravelling the fibres of their long years together had been desperately painful. Now their home and all its contents had been sold off and they were going their separate ways.

The auction sale was almost over when the final item came up for sale – a little tin box of no obvious intrinsic value. But Bob held up his hand. "No, that's not for sale," he said, and he took the tin box away. The sale was over. Bob went off in one direction and Pauline in another.

Years passed. The day came when Bob and Pauline's granddaughter was to be married. They both came to the wedding, seeing each other again for the first time in years. Time had softened the anger, lessened the hurt, and dissolved any remaining bitterness. Soon after the wedding, Bob invited Pauline back to his place and they had a cup of tea together. Pauline looked round the room, and remarked, "You've still got that old tin box."

Bob got the box down from the shelf and opened it. There was nothing in it, and there was everything in it. "It's my box of memories," he said. "When I feel sad, I open the box and take out a memory, and it helps. Of course no one else can see my memories… except you," he added. "You would recognize them all."

There was a pause while they sat together in companionable silence, and then the memories began to flow out of the old tin box. "Do you remember when we first took the children to see the ocean? When we moved into our first home? What about that time when we lost the keys? When we couldn't get the car to start? And can you remember how thrilled we were when our granddaughter was born?"

And so it continued. The day wore on. Evening fell. They were still sitting there in the twilight, taking out their memories, savouring them together, so grateful to find that they had remained intact in the old tin box.

And the strange thing was, the old tin box seemed to keep only the happy memories. The unhappy times were no longer in focus, no longer of importance.

When night came and they were about to say goodbye again, Pauline gave Bob a hug. "You know what," she said. "I think today we finished a chapter of our life together, and wrote the first sentence of a whole new chapter – a different chapter, with a different story, but still a story that will be written with love."

Retelling of a story by Edward Hays

The wisdom of the scar

A respected member of the tribe was grieving deeply for the loss of his only son, who had been killed by an enemy's arrow. The people urged him to seek help from the medicine man for his terrible grieving, and so one day he sought him out.

"You will carry the wound of this grief for always," said the medicine man, "but you will also heal, with the passage of time. My counsel is this: go into the forest and choose a tall sturdy tree. This tree is a symbol of yourself. Now take your axe and strike the tree, making a gash in its bark. Then go home and nurse your grief for a year, and then return to the tree. Put your hand into the gash you have made, and notice how it is just beginning to close a little. Go back to the tree every year. Place your hand in the gash each time, and remember your lost son as you do so."

The grieving father followed the counsel of the medicine man. Each year he went back, feeling compassion for the tree he had wounded, and even beginning to feel compassion towards himself. Each year the gash in the tree had closed a bit more. Time passed, and eventually the gash in the tree had become just a faint scar. And every year the man's grief became just a little less bitter, and a little more bearable.

Years later he returned to the medicine man to thank him for his counsel. "I have not only learned that time will heal the deepest hurt, but I have learned to be compassionate towards the trees, towards my brothers and sisters in the tribe, and towards myself. Perhaps I can even begin to forgive the man who killed my son. But I think there will always be a scar on my heart, just as there will always be a scar on the tree I hurt."

"That will be so," said the medicine man. "But let that scar remind you not only that you have been hurt, but also that you have been healed."

Retelling of a Native American story

Trench warfare

There were once two neighbours who farmed adjacent lands. They had once been friends but they had quarrelled bitterly and now they refused to speak to each other.

One day the Spirit of Spite flew down and whispered in one neighbour's ear: "Let's dig a deep trench between your land and your neighbour's so that he can never get across to your side." And so this was duly done. The other neighbour watched angrily as this deep wide trench sliced the land decisively in two.

The Spirit of Spite, pleased with his work, then went to the other neighbour and whispered in his ear: "See what a spiteful thing your neighbour has done. Let's build a high fence between your two properties so that you no longer have to see his farm from your window." And so the second neighbour called on a travelling carpenter to come and build a fence.

When the carpenter arrived he could see at once where the problem lay. Taking the planks of wood, the nails, the hammer, and the saw that the farmer gave him, he set about his task while the farmer went to market.

But when the farmer returned in the evening he found not a fence but a bridge, not only firmly constructed across the trench, but even lovingly carved and finished.

Before he could protest, to his great astonishment he saw his neighbour approaching across the bridge, hand outstretched. "After my spiteful action in digging this trench between us," the neighbour said, "you have offered friendship in the form of this beautiful bridge. Let us shake hands and let bygones be bygones, and from now on we shall be not just neighbours but friends."

And then they noticed the carpenter who was walking off into the distance. They called after him and invited him to stay for supper. "I would love to," he replied, "but I must move on. I have many more bridges to build." And with that he was gone.

Source unknown

Love and Compassion

A little word of praise

There was once a little word of praise. She longed to grow into something big and strong, but her mother would stroke her little head and say, "I'm afraid you'll always be little, but never forget – a little word of praise is greater and stronger than the most powerful word of command."

As she wandered through the world, she was nearly knocked over one morning by a man who was rushing to get to the office on time. She hitched a ride on the corner of his briefcase, and sat down quietly on the edge of his desk. Appalled, she listened as he vented his bad temper on the people who worked for him. "Why are you late?" he asked one unfortunate colleague. "One more late morning and you needn't bother coming in again."

"Get that job done now," he barked at another. "It's way overdue."

"Get me a fresh coffee," he growled at his secretary. "This one's cold!"

Then he heard a little voice from the corner of his desk: "Excuse me, sir, but could you use a little word of praise?"

"Praise!" he grumbled. "Whatever for? These people are here to work and make money for me. Praise isn't any use for anything." And the little word of praise swallowed hard, and moved on.

A little further on she found her way in through the open window of a big house. In the kitchen a woman was running backwards and forwards trying frantically to cook a meal while shouting at three unruly children who flatly refused to do what she told them.

"Move those toys away immediately!" she bawled at one of them.

"Get on with your homework," she bellowed at another.

"One more squeak and you'll go to bed without any supper," she threatened the third.

The little word of praise was distressed by all this turmoil. "Excuse me," she ventured, to the woman, "but could you use a little word of praise?"

"What's that?" the woman retorted angrily. "What I need is three pairs of hands and a big stick to keep these terrible children in order. Now get out of my kitchen!"

And the little word of praise wiped a tear from her cheek, and moved on.

Eventually she came to a school. She slipped into a classroom and sat down in a quiet corner on the teacher's desk. The children in the classroom were not very happy. Some were even crying. The teacher had nothing but criticism for their work. Our little friend listened, aghast, as the teacher barked out her orders. "Sit up straight! Stop fidgeting! Stand over there in the corner! Get on with your work! Be quiet!"

And then something remarkable happened. The teacher was silent for a few moments. She thought she had heard a gentle whisper in her ear. "Excuse me," it had said, "but could you use a little word of praise?"

It was as though suddenly the sun had come out again. The children couldn't believe their ears.

"Your writing is improving very well, David."

"What a lovely painting, Bridget; your parents will be so proud when they see it."

"Jamie, you've been a real help to me today. Thank you!"

The little word of praise was delighted. She watched, entranced, as each little face relaxed and began to shine again. The classroom felt warmer. The air felt fresher. Happiness had moved in.

She ran home to her mother and told her about the day's adventures.

"Well, there you are, dear," her mother smiled. "You may be very little, but you are stronger than all those big commands. You are strong enough to make the sun rise in people's hearts."

Retelling of a traditional German folk story

A star is born

Robbie was never brilliant at sport. He played a very mediocre game of football, and he was never going to be a star. He guessed he was always going to be just a reserve. But he was happy to go along to all the games, cheer on his teammates, and do his bit when they called for him. And always Granddad would be there too, encouraging him, praising his efforts, assuring him that he would be a great player if he just kept at it.

Robbie was twelve years old when his beloved granddad died. The boy was inconsolable. It seemed to be an impossibility that the granddad who was always there for him had gone, would never be there on the touchline again urging him on.

There was an important school match just two days after Granddad's funeral. No one expected Robbie to show up. Everyone knew about his loss. So the surprise was great when Robbie was right there, in his football strip, sitting on the touchline, watching the game, thinking of Granddad… thinking, thinking…

A sudden shout interrupted his reverie. Something had happened on the pitch. One of the team was injured, and they were carrying him off on a stretcher. Robbie barely took it in. And then another shout. "Robbie! … Ready?" And something clicked into place in Robbie's mind. He stood up and walked onto the field.

And Robbie ran as he had never run before, fleet as a mountain goat. And he passed the ball as he had never done before, with deadly accuracy. And then, three minutes before the final whistle, he scored the decisive winning goal.

Robbie was carried off the pitch that day too – not on a stretcher, but on the shoulders of his exultant teammates. Afterwards the coach came and shook his hand. "Well done, lad," he said. "You played like a pro. At this rate we'll be having you in the first team. Whatever got into you today, boy? I've never seen you play like that before."

"I guess it was Granddad," Robbie said, almost inaudibly.

"Ah, yes," said the coach. "We're all real sorry about your granddad, son. Just sorry he couldn't be here to see you now."

"But that's the thing," said Robbie. "You see, my granddad was blind. And now that he's in heaven, this is the first time he's actually been able to *see* me play. I had to give him my best – my very best. And I always will."

Source unknown

Charlie's coat

Charlie was a cross between a llama and an alpaca. He knew he wasn't quite the real thing when both the llamas and the alpacas in the zoo refused to have anything to do with him. It wasn't a very happy life in the zoo. The llamas always clustered together and shared their secrets, and so did the alpacas, and there wasn't much love lost between the two groups of animals. But they all agreed on one thing. Neither group was going to accept a mixed-up neither-nor sort of a creature like Charlie.

Charlie didn't even have a name in the zoo. Even the zoo managers didn't want him, and so everyone was delighted when a local infants' school offered to have Charlie for the children to play with. So Charlie went off to his new life, still full of trepidation, but things could hardly get worse, he thought.

In fact things got very much better. The children were kind to Charlie. They didn't know he was a mixed-up kind of creature. And one little boy in particular, a boy called Jimmie, spent a lot of time with Charlie. He learned how to groom him and how to feed him. Jimmie knew something of how it feels to be not-quite-acceptable. He had no father and lived with his mother and older brother, and there was no money to spare for any extras. Jimmie always came to school in old hand-me-down clothes. So talking to Charlie and caring for him every day was Jimmie's great joy. He was sure that Charlie understood what he was saying. Even more importantly, he was sure Charlie understood what he *wasn't* saying – the things he couldn't put into words, the silent longing and aching in his heart. Charlie understood. Jimmie was sure of it.

One day the shearers came to town, and Jimmie looked on in horror as they sheared off all of Charlie's coat. All the time it was happening, Jimmie wouldn't take his eyes away from his friend. And Charlie's big brown eyes gazed back at him, as if to reassure him: "Don't fret for me, little friend. My coat will grow again." But the shearers were less kind.

"This old creature's coat is worthless," they said. "He's neither a llama nor an alpaca. We can't sell this wool to anyone." And so Charlie's coat was thrown aside on the floor, and Jimmie's heart was breaking.

After the shearers had gone, a teacher came and picked up the abandoned fleece. At first she was going to dispose of it, but then she had another thought. "We could spin this wool, and show the children how spinning works," she reflected.

And so over the next few weeks the children learned how wool is spun, using Charlie's old coat. Gradually his wool turned into soft brown yarn and was made into a warm jacket. The children were thrilled to see this happen, and everyone wanted to wear the new warm brown jacket.

And when it was finished, the teacher gathered all the children together, and told them her decision. "We have all enjoyed seeing how Charlie's old coat has been transformed into a new jacket just big enough for a little boy. I think Charlie would want to give this new jacket to the little boy who has faithfully and lovingly cared for him all through the year. This jacket is for you, Jimmie."

And the children all clapped, and Jimmie glowed with pride and joy, hardly believing his luck. And then he went straight over to Charlie, and flung his arms around the animal's neck and thanked him. And Charlie gazed silently at his little friend, and those big brown eyes seemed to say thank you too: "You have looked after me, and now I will look after you. This is life's great circle of caring and sharing, loving and giving."

Margaret Silf

Finding love

There was once a very pretty girl, who lived all alone. Many boys wanted to marry her, but she was always afraid that they really loved her only for her beauty and not for herself, so she always refused.

One day the devil heard about this girl and decided to fetch her for himself, to brighten hell up a bit. One day he knocked at her door, disguised as a beggar. Being a kind-hearted girl, she let him in, but once inside her cottage he threw off his disguise with a puff of smoke and confronted her. The girl, of course, was terrified.

"I've come to take you to hell," he announced.

But she refused. "You can't force me to come with you," she told him.

"True," said the devil. "I can't take you before your time without your consent. But if you come with me, you will be far and away the prettiest girl there."

"But I'm already the prettiest girl *here*," she retorted.

"Right," conceded the devil. "But in hell your beauty will last for ever and will never fade."

The girl hesitated at this suggestion, tempted by the thought of immortal beauty. Then she remembered that what she really desired was not beauty, but love.

"Is there any love in hell?" she asked the devil.

To this question, of course, the devil had no satisfactory answer. In his frustration he cast around for another way forward. He knew that he could not take the girl, but he *could* take her beauty. And so he vanished again, in a cloud of smoke, carrying her beauty away with him.

Two years passed, and the devil had still not forgotten the girl. Curious to see how she was getting along without her beauty, he went back to earth. There, in her cottage, he found an ugly woman, with an ugly man beside her, and an equally ugly baby in the cradle between them. But there was such an aura of love around their table and their fireside that he reeled back in shock. She had finally found what she had always longed for.

Retelling of a story by Natalie Babbitt

The angel's kiss

Little Maria was born with a cleft palate. She lived in a poor country, and there were no doctors nearby to help her. So she grew up with a very distorted face, unable to drink properly or even to smile. The other children made fun of her, and even many of the grown-ups seemed uncomfortable around her. She felt very lonely and unloved.

But one day a new teacher arrived at the village school. Everyone loved her. She was so pretty and so kind, and all the children wanted to please her. But Maria stayed back, out of sight as far as possible, afraid that this teacher too would not want to be near her.

Time passed, and the new teacher seemed to be at ease with everyone, including Maria, yet Maria found it hard to trust. She remained defensive and withdrawn. Until one day when the teacher asked the children to write a story about themselves.

Maria didn't know what to write. The story of her life was not a nice one. But perhaps she could make it into a better story. So at the end of class she gave the teacher a new story: "There was once a little girl who was born ugly, and no one could do anything about it. No one liked her. No one would play with her. But one day an angel came to visit her as she slept. The angel bent over the little girl, so lovingly, and kissed her brow. And when she woke the next morning the little girl looked in the mirror, and saw that she was beautiful. The angel's kiss had transformed her overnight and she lived happily ever after."

That night the teacher read the stories the children had written. And as she read Maria's story, a tear fell from her eyes. The next day she handed the stories back to the children, and Maria took her story back, expecting a bad mark. But, instead, she found this message written at the bottom of the page: "Maria, I wish you were my little girl," the teacher had written. But the words were a bit smudged, where the teacher's tear had fallen.

And from that day onwards, Maria knew that her dream had come true, and an angel really had kissed her, and she would never be the same again.

Retelling of a traditional story

The bishop's ring

There was once a little girl who grew up in Canada. Her mother was a Celt from Scotland. Her father was of the Cree nation. They raised her and her siblings lovingly, but they were never a rich family.

When she grew up the girl felt called by God to become a priest and go out to serve those who lived on the edges of society. She ministered lovingly to them in her own quiet way, seeing herself as living on the edge with those she served, and certainly not in the centre of the church or the world. No one could have been more surprised, therefore, when she was elected to be a bishop.

Now, as you know, a bishop wears a special ring in token of his or her office. This newly elected bishop, however, had no money to spare for luxuries. All she had was a beautiful amethyst stone, but when she took it to the jeweller to have it set in gold, he quoted a price far beyond anything her family could afford. "And, in any case," he warned her, "this stone has an impurity in it. It is flawed."

Now when the new bishop told her family about the jeweller's verdict, they quietly went about solving the problem. Everyone contributed what bit of gold they could find around their homes. Broken earrings, a segment of a gold chain, even a gold filling from a tooth. All these offerings arrived – the broken, the neglected, the cast-aside. All were gladly given. And when the jeweller was given these gold offerings, he melted them down and created a beautiful setting for the amethyst. When it was finished he engraved it with a symbol of Celtic spirituality and a symbol of indigenous Cree spirituality. And inside the new ring he incorporated the ring her father had given to her mother on their wedding day, with its blessing of continuity and love.

The bishop wears her ring with pride and humility – proud to belong to her natural and her wider spiritual families, and humbled to recall, every day, that she is called to gather the broken, the neglected and the cast-aside and invite them into something new and beautiful, while never forgetting that, like the amethyst, she is also flawed and in need of the eternal jeweller.

Margaret Silf

The blacksmith

Once a village blacksmith had a vision. The angel of the Lord came to him and said, "The Lord has sent me. The time has come for you to take up your abode in his kingdom."

"I thank God for thinking of me," said the blacksmith, "but, as you know, the season for sowing crops will soon be here. The people of the village will need their ploughs repaired and their horses shod. I don't want to seem ungrateful, but do you think I might put off taking up my abode in the kingdom until I've finished?"

The angel looked at him in the wise and loving way of angels. "I'll see what can be done," he said, and he vanished.

The blacksmith continued with his work and was almost finished when he heard of a neighbour who had fallen ill right in the middle of the planting season. The next time he saw the angel, the blacksmith pointed towards the barren fields and pleaded with the angel, "Do you think eternity can hold off a little longer? If I don't finish the job, my friend's family will suffer." Again the angel smiled and vanished. The blacksmith's friend recovered, but another's barn burned down and a third was deep in sorrow at the death of his wife, and the fourth… and so on.

Whenever the angel reappeared, the blacksmith just spread his hands in a gesture of resignation and compassion and drew the angel's eyes to where the sufferings were.

One evening the blacksmith began to think about the angel and how he'd put him off for such a long time. Suddenly he felt very old and tired and said, "Lord, if you would like to send your angel again, I think I would like to see him now."

He'd no sooner spoken than the angel stood before him. "If you still want to take me," said the blacksmith, "I am now ready to take up my place in the kingdom of the Lord."

And the angel looked at the blacksmith in surprise and smiled, and said, "Where do you think you have been all these years?"

Retelling of a story by Jack McArdle

The disappearing rabbi

There was once a kind and compassionate rabbi who was in the habit of disappearing every week on the eve of the Sabbath. Every week the congregation wondered where he had gone. "Perhaps he is secretly meeting with God," they speculated, "ascending the mountain like Moses before him."

One day their curiosity got the better of them and one man from the congregation secretly followed the rabbi. He found him disguised in peasant's clothing, helping an old, paralysed Gentile woman to clean her cottage and prepare a Sabbath meal.

When the man returned to the congregation, they asked him, "Tell us, where does he go every week? Does he ascend the holy mountain?"

"No," replied the man. "He goes higher than that."

Retelling of a story by Anthony de Mello

The jacket that came home

One day there was a knock at the monastery door. The monk who responded found a derelict-looking mendicant on the doorstep, wearing just a thin shirt and a pair of ragged trousers on this bitterly cold day.

"Good day to you, Father," said the beggar. "I wonder, would you have a warm jacket to spare at all? I've no home and it's awfully cold right now, living on the streets."

The monk immediately took pity on the poor shivering man. "Just wait a moment," he said, and went to his room, where his own one and only jacket was hanging on the door hook.

Minutes later he was back at the door and he gave the homeless man his jacket, with no thought as to how he himself would keep warm when he had to go outside. "He needs it more than I do," he thought to himself.

A few weeks later the monks were sitting together over supper one night and the subject of homeless people came up. "There was one round here only yesterday," said one of the monks. "I gave him my jacket."

Then another monk remembered, "The same thing happened to me only last week." One after the other the monks recalled how a homeless man had come to the door begging for a jacket, and one after another of them had given away their own jacket. There seemed to be a veritable epidemic of men in need of jackets this winter.

It was nearly Christmas. The first monk was down in the town, in the market square, when he was surprised to see the homeless man who had begged him for a jacket. There he was running a nice little business in the market, selling the monks' jackets. But he said nothing and passed by with a wry smile on his face.

Others were happy too. There were many in the town who had no warm clothes. One old man, for example, was overjoyed to be able to buy a good jacket so cheaply. He paid for it and put it on straight away and then made his way back home. But he didn't get far before he was stopped in his tracks by the sight of a man lying at the edge of the road, where he had been taken ill and collapsed. He couldn't have known that the casualty had been on his way home to the monastery. He couldn't have known that the bystanders had already called an ambulance. All he knew was that here was a man shivering in the road, sick, cold and helpless. Without hesitation he took off the jacket he had just bought, and laid it gently around the man. "He needs it more than I do," he thought to himself.

And so it was that the jacket that had been given away so freely all those weeks ago found its way home to its original owner, carried on a tide of deception and generosity, of need and of compassion.

Margaret Silf

The memory quilt

There was once a family comprising parents and seven sisters, and a beloved grandmother who lived in a nearby village. There was very little money in the family, and so the girls grew up learning how to make things out of nothing and never to waste anything.

The years passed and their grandma's seventieth birthday came around. The girls wanted to give her a very special gift, and wondered what to choose, and how to procure it.

Then they had a great idea. After all these years, they noticed, Grandma's bed quilt was getting very worn and faded. If they all worked together, they thought, they could make a new one. So they put all their savings together to buy new material to make the quilt, and decided to make it as close as possible in appearance and design to the old, worn-out quilt which had served her so well for so long.

After several months of work, the quilt was half-finished. It was a very close reconstruction of the old quilt, and the material had cost them all their savings. But the quilt also needed a lining on its underside, to make it soft and warm. And there was no money left to buy any suitable material for this lining.

The sisters were very disappointed. They had dreamed of making the underside as beautiful in its way as the top of the quilt, but this was proving impossible. Then one of them had an idea.

"There is simply no way that we can buy any nice silk to make the underside beautiful," she admitted. "What I suggest is this. If each of us searches in our cupboards to find remnants of material, we could at least sew these pieces of leftovers together, so that we can finish off the quilt. After all, no one will see the underside of the quilt, and Grandma will understand."

And so they searched in their cupboards and found the remnants of old clothes they had worn as children, and even their dolls' clothes from childhood. Carefully they cut up these remnants and sewed them lovingly into a patchwork lining for the new quilt.

Grandma's birthday dawned, and she was delighted with her new quilt. The girls insisted on putting it on the bed straight away. It looked just like the old quilt, but fresh and new. Grandma would sleep well under it, they were sure.

Imagine their shock, therefore, when they visited Grandma a few days later and discovered that she had turned the quilt the other way up.

"Grandma," they protested, "you've got the quilt the wrong way round. The underside is just a makeshift mixture of remnants we sewed together to make the lining, because we had run out of the good cloth."

"But, my dear girls," said Grandma, "when I turned your beautiful quilt over and saw all those bits and pieces of cloth, they brought back so many happy memories. The brown cloth was part of the skirt you wore, Mary, when you first started school. And this indigo material was your apron, Jane, when you were first learning to cook in my kitchen when you were seven years old. And, if I'm not mistaken, this bright yellow piece was from a dress of your favourite doll, Linda. And this blue-checked patch was surely your first school blouse, Rosie? Look at this stripy piece. Isn't this from your old pyjamas, Susy? And I'll never forget this pink taffeta that came from your party dress when you had your eighth birthday, Kate. And, see, here is some green silk that your granddad brought home from market one day, which we made into a dancing tunic for you, Becky. And look at this," she said, pointing to a fluffy white piece with tears of joy in her eyes. "This was part of the blanket you all used when you were just babies."

The girls fell silent. And Grandma's memories kept on pouring out as she remembered the story behind every piece of the quilt lining.

"You couldn't have given me any greater gift than this," she said finally. "The quilt will keep my body warm every night, and these happy memories will warm my heart whenever I feel lonely. That's why I turned it the other way up."

Margaret Silf

The shoemaker's story

One cold winter day a weary, hungry traveller was passing through a crowded city. Hoping for something to eat, he knocked on the door of a rich man. The house was lit up and warm and he could see someone close the curtains against him, but no one answered the door. He knocked again. The light in the house went out, and there was no further response. Appealing in vain for help one last time, the traveller went on his way.

A passer-by noticed this incident and warned the traveller that this rich man would never give anything away. Instead, he directed the stranger to the home of the local shoemaker, who was well known for his generosity. And there, in the shoemaker's humble dwelling, the traveller was welcomed. He met the shoemaker's family and shared their meal, entertaining them with his traveller's tales. When night fell, he slept on the floor by the fire, and when he left the next morning the shoemaker gave him two silver coins for the road.

Time passed, and eventually the rich man died. No one cared. Everyone regarded him as a mean and heartless neighbour. People kept on going to the shoemaker, however, whenever they needed help, but they noticed that he no longer invited them in or offered them his customary hospitality. The local pastor noticed this change, and one day he asked the shoemaker what had happened to change his attitude.

The shoemaker admitted that actually he barely had enough to feed his own family. His former generosity had been possible only because the rich man had always been watching out for any sign of someone in need. When he had noticed someone with a problem he had brought the shoemaker the means to help them. But he never wanted anyone to know of his secret generosity, in case he should become proud.

After hearing the shoemaker's story, and the truth about the deceased rich man, the pastor called the townspeople together to tell them the truth. He told them that many people were now living good and happy lives because of the rich man's secret kindness. And, from that day onwards, day after day, flowers and tributes appeared on the rich man's grave.

Retelling of a story by Lorraine Hartin-Gelardi

The three sisters

In a field far away there grew a fine plant called Sister Corn. As the sun shone down through the summer months she grew tall and strong, but in the hot weather the earth became dry so that her feet hurt. She grew weary and she needed to take a lot of strength out of the soil just to keep on growing.

Now Sister Squash noticed what was happening and lay down at the feet of Sister Corn to cool the earth and soothe her sister's pain, and bring moisture to the parched ground by helping to prevent evaporation. However, Sister Corn noticed that Sister Squash was not getting any of the rainwater that fell into her own heart, so she bent her outer leaves over, to channel some of the precious water down to Sister Squash. In return, Sister Squash used her spikiness to keep predators away from them both.

Nearby in the vegetable bed grew Sister Bean. Now Sister Bean was weak and could not support her own weight, and so she climbed up the strong stem of Sister Corn. In return she was able to fix nitrogen in her roots to make the soil more fertile for next year's corn crop, and she helped Sister Corn stand firm against the days when the strong winds blew.

And when harvest time came, each of the three sisters brought her own special gift to the table. Sister Corn provided carbohydrates, Sister Squash gave vitamins in her fruit and oil from her seeds, and Sister Bean brought protein and amino acids.

And, together, the three sisters brought the world a lesson in how to live and work in mutual co-operation.

Retelling of a traditional Iroquois legend

The traveller and the stone

A good and wise woman once lived in the mountains. She knew how to read the winds and the clouds, knew how the weather would be, and conversed with the birds and the animals.

One day as she was walking along the mountain trail her gaze was caught by a large round stone. She picked it up and rubbed it in her hands, noticing its amazing beauty, and instinctively knew that it must be a precious stone.

The next day she met a young traveller along the path. He stopped to ask her for directions and they fell into conversation. He couldn't help noticing that she had a large round stone in her basket, and he admired it.

"Please have it if it pleases you so much," she offered.

And so the traveller took the stone, thanking her, and went on his way. Delighted with his acquisition, he asked a jeweller to look at it, and was told that it was in fact a valuable amethyst. At first he was overjoyed at his luck in being given this stone. But the more he thought about it, the less comfortable he felt. Eventually he made his way back to the mountain and found the woman's humble lodge.

"I have brought back the stone you gave me," he said. "Perhaps you didn't know that it was valuable. I really can't keep it, knowing this. It wouldn't be right."

"Come in, young friend," she said, "and let me make you a cup of mountain tea." Then, as they sat together with their tea, she continued, "My friend, I knew the stone was valuable. But you loved it so much I was happy for you to have it."

Amazed at her generosity, and sensing that she was a woman of extraordinary wisdom, he was speechless. The woman broke the silence. "But, if you really don't want to keep the stone," she said, "is there perhaps something else I might give you instead, as a mark of our friendship?"

Her guest thought for a while before replying. "Well, yes," he said quietly. "Would you perhaps give me a fragment of the precious gift that is in your heart that makes you so wise and so generous? For that would be of far greater value than any stone."

Source unknown

To be a brother

A poor boy from the ghetto was fascinated to see a man drive up the street in a big, shiny, brand-new sports car. He just couldn't take his eyes off the man and his car. The car's owner noticed this intense interest and became suspicious. Was this urchin planning to damage the car, or even perhaps to steal it?

So he approached the boy, intending to warn him off. But, before he could say anything, the boy burst out with his burning question: "Sir, how did you get such an amazing car?"

"Now look here, kid, it's none of your business, and don't you dare touch my car! But, if you must know, my brother gave it to me."

The boy's jaw dropped in amazement.

The man was thinking, "I bet he's wishing he could have a brother like that."

But the boy replied, "Oh my! How I wish I could be a brother like that."

Source unknown

Triplets

Once there were twin girls, called Faith and Hope. The twins, though they were very close, were also very different. Faith was a sweet child, but she tended to be fussy, always wore her Sunday clothes, and was a rather weak and ailing infant. Hope, on the other hand, was a wild child, more sturdy than her sister, but unpredictable and likely to run out just when she was needed.

The years passed, and Faith and Hope grew old. Faith by now had become much stronger, but she was rather stiff-limbed and rigid and tended to be a bit judgmental. Hope, by contrast, had become weak, and was very close to fading away completely.

Then one day there was a knock at their door, and there stood an angel, holding a stranger by the hand.

"I have a surprise for you," the angel said. "You have always believed you were twins, but actually you have a sister whom you have never known. You are triplets, and this is your third sister. Her name is Love."

Faith and Hope were overjoyed to discover their long-lost sister and they welcomed her into their home. Gradually they got to know each other. And Love helped Faith to become more relaxed and compassionate, and she helped Hope to grow stronger and more reliable. And still they continue to live side by side. Faith, Hope, and Love, but the wisest and the most enduring of the three is Love.

Margaret Silf

Trust and Fear

Adventures of a puddle-fish

There was once a big tree growing beside the river. Every year after the wet season, a puddle would get left behind in the hollow formed by the tree's roots. And every year a small school of puddle-fish would settle in this puddle. There they spent all their time swimming in circles, trying to catch water-bugs, and fighting over what they caught.

Then one day there was a huge splash, and a brightly coloured rainbow-fish flopped into the puddle, after leaping out of the river below.

The puddle-fish, shocked by this new arrival, all huddled at the side of the pool and waited, carefully observing the newcomer. The big fish seemed to glow with iridescence, and he was *smiling*.

One bold puddle-fish made a move towards him. "Who are you? Where are you from?" he asked.

"I come from the ocean," came the reply.

"What is 'ocean'?" the puddle-fish asked.

"Well," said the rainbow-fish, "ocean is… ocean is… it's what we're made for. It goes on for ever. It's full of so many wonderful creatures. It's brimming with movement and life."

"How do you get there?" asked the puddle-fish, eager to discover this new wonder.

"You just jump out of the puddle, and trust the river to carry you there," the rainbow-fish assured him.

But it was then that the objections began to rise up from the ranks of the puddle-fish.

The realist-fish objected: "This puddle is reality. You are deluded about the ocean."

The scaredy-fish whimpered: "No one would ever dare make that leap into the great unknown."

The political-fish proposed: "Both sides of the argument have merit. We should form a discussion group and talk it through."

"Talking won't get you to the ocean," the rainbow fish warned them gently. "And summer is coming. Soon this little puddle will dry up, and then what?"

Eventually the visiting fish leapt back into the river and swam away.

And, very tentatively, a few brave puddle-fish also took the leap of faith. The others gazed after them with pity, and went back to swimming round in circles, hunting for water-bugs, and fighting over what they caught.

Retelling of a traditional story

Arms race

There was once a tribe of people who lived in a cave high on a hillside. There they hunted for food, gathered the fruits that the earth yielded, cared for their children, listened to the wisdom of the elders, struggled, loved, and laughed together. They thought they were the only people on earth. They had no fears. They had no enemies.

It happened that one day some people from a different tribe came through the valley. They too were looking for a cave to make into a home. All they desired was a place to hunt and gather food. Their whole ambition was to live and love and laugh together, raise their children and honour the elders. The world, after all, was a very big place.

When the first group of cave-dwellers saw these unexpected arrivals, they began to wonder: who are these people? What do they want here? Can we trust them?

And then, just in case these newcomers should prove to be hostile, they began to build a pile of stones with which to defend themselves if the strangers from across the valley should one day attack them.

The new arrivals, in their turn, looked across the valley and there on the opposite hillside they saw the growing pile of stones. The people here seemed to be very warlike. Were they intending to attack them with those stones? How should they defend themselves if they did?

So they too began to build up a pile of stones.

And the people of the first tribe began to mutter to each other, "See, didn't we know it? These newcomers are hostile. They are piling up stones to attack us. We should build our pile of stones even higher."

And so it went on, each group adding more and more stones to their pile, their mutual distrust growing greater every day.

Until eventually the piles of stones were so high that neither tribe could see the faces of their neighbours any longer. All they could see was an enemy.

Margaret Silf

Autumn assembly

It was autumn in the woods. Most of the leaves had already fallen, and were lying on the frosty grass feeling rather sorry for themselves. Others were resting in halfway houses, on the branches of the conifers, waiting to see what would happen next. It was time for the autumn assembly, when Mother Nature, their beloved head teacher, would address them all. There was an atmosphere of anticipation and a degree of anxiety in the air. Mother Nature very rarely called them all together for a pep talk. She usually communicated with them quietly and individually, in the silent recesses of their hearts, guiding them in the ways of life. But the autumn assembly was different.

"My children," she began, "you are probably wondering why I have called you together, and what is going to happen now that you have fallen from your trees." There was a rustle of assent. "Now you remember that half a year ago you were just sprouting. Then, everything centred on *you*. We all told you how fresh and green and beautiful you were. We did everything to help you grow and blossom. But now, you are entering the next stage of your lives. It may look to you like dying, but actually it is a new beginning. Now, as you lie here on the ground, you are learning to let go of your separate existence, beautiful though that has been, in order to contribute to a bigger story, for all my creation. I am going to gather you all together now to make a blanket for the earth, to keep her warm and sheltered through the cold winter months. Beneath that blanket the new seeds will begin to germinate for next year's springtime. You yourselves will appear to disintegrate into the ground, but actually I will be transforming you into nourishment for the next generation. In this way you will live for ever.

"And there is one more thing I ask of you," she continued. "I want you to be an example to my human children. They don't always listen to my wisdom as you do. They too spend the first half of their lives centred mainly on becoming the individual person they can be. And then the later years come, and they too have to let go, and surrender to the call to become part of a greater whole, a greater good. They find that hard. In your autumn days, you have a great deal to teach them."

As she spoke, the rabbits and the squirrels were listening too, and a flock of geese flew overhead. "See," she added, "these other children of mine are learning the same life lesson, and they are also an example to the human children. See how in northern regions the rabbit gradually relinquishes the rich colour of his fur, to turn white so that he will be safe from predators in the snow. See how the squirrels prepare for hard times by saving and storing what they need, not by recklessly spending it as so many of the human children do. See the geese – how, when the time is right and they have raised their young, they let go of the old familiar ways and places, and fly forth trustfully into the unknown. All these have much to teach the human children. And you, my beautiful fallen leaves, you too are part of this great lesson. Trust me now, and let me fold you to my heart and transform you into winter's blanket."

And one by one the leaves settled down into the arms of their dear mother, and consented to be part of the bigger story.

Margaret Silf

Johnny Appleseed

Little Johnny is sitting in the kitchen with his mum. On the table is a bowl of apples. Johnny takes an apple in his hands and gazes at it with unconcealed curiosity.

Turning to Mum, he asks, "Where do apples come from?"

"From an apple tree," she replies. "There are some in the orchard."

"But where do apple trees come from?" he persists.

"They grow from apple seeds in the soil in the orchard."

"And where do the apple seeds come from?" Johnny demands to know.

"They live inside the apple," Mum explains.

There is a long silence while Johnny ponders this conundrum.

If the apple seed lives inside the apple and the apple comes from an apple seed, by what kind of magic or miracle does the apple seed get out of the apple?

"How does the apple seed get to the orchard?" he asks finally.

"Well," says Mum, "first the apple has to die. It has to get eaten, or it has to fall into the earth and rot, so that the seed can get out and start a new life."

Another long and thoughtful pause. Then…

"Does everything have to die?" asks Johnny brightly.

"It does if it wants to live," says Mum.

Margaret Silf

Leaving the nest

The eagle pair had built their nest high on the mountain crags. First they made a sturdy foundation of twigs and small branches on the bare rock. Then they worked a more finely woven layer inside. And finally they lined the nest with their own feathers. And then the mother eagle laid her eggs, and brooded over them until they were ready to hatch.

When the tiny chicks hatched they nestled in the warmth and the comfort of the feather-lined nest. And time passed and they grew bigger, and were ready to leave the nest and learn to fly and make their own lives.

One by one the small eagles were persuaded to leave the nest. But one was reluctant to go. The nest was so comfortable and he really wanted to live there for ever.

So the parent eagles tried to persuade him to move out. First they removed the cosy layer of feathers. But still he would not leave. Then they removed the layer of fine grass and twigs. But still he would not leave. And then in desperation they removed the entire outer nest, leaving him perched on the bare rock. But still he would not fly.

And, finally, they took their fledgling to the edge of the high crag, and pushed him off...

... and then they flew close below him, to catch him lest he fall.

Margaret Silf

Night ordeal

A young Native American boy was entering into his initiation rites, as the first step into manhood. He was sent out into the forest one night and blindfolded, to pass the night alone and confront his fears.

The night passed so very slowly. Every small sound, every rustle in the undergrowth, intensified his terror. What wild creatures might be lurking all around him, and he would not be able to see them through his blindfold? Worse, the fears of the supernatural came to haunt him. What spirits might be abroad, and he would not know how to banish them? And, worst of all, an awareness of deep solitude invaded his heart and paralysed him with fear. Never in his young life had he been so alone, so defenceless, so utterly exposed.

When dawn finally broke and one of the elders came to remove the boy's blindfold, his relief was palpable. And the very first thing he saw, sitting there alert among the nearby trees, was his own father. He had been there all night, just a few yards away from his son, watching over him with a father's love, and now rising and walking towards him to embrace him with a father's pride.

Retelling of a Native American story

Samuel Seed

Once upon a time a little seed called Samuel fell onto a patch of land where there happened to be a bit of space.

At first Samuel made enemies, because before he could begin to sprout he took a great deal out of the earth. The other plants grumbled about him: "This newcomer is taking moisture and nutrients from the earth and beams of energy from the sun that rightfully belong to us," they complained.

They all resented Samuel, until one day a miracle happened. Samuel began to transform the place where he had landed. The soil began to break up around him and became more alive than it had been before. A tiny new shoot began to push through the earth, and then a plant, leaves, flowers, and more seeds. The air became fragrant with the scent of Samuel's new flowers. The butterflies came.

Eventually his leaves died and fell to the earth again, giving back the nutrients they had borrowed, and the sun smiled down on the patch of land and blessed Samuel, who had fulfilled his purpose, and transformed the place where he had landed.

Margaret Silf

Stepping stones

The "woman of the woods", as she was known by the folk who lived nearby, had lived since time immemorial in her cosy little cottage by the river. No one rightly knew how old she was, or when she had first come to live by the riverside. Everyone got on well with her and respected her age and her wisdom. But she herself had a restless soul. She knew – perhaps she had really *always* known – that there was something important she had still to discover. The more she pondered this mystery, the more she realized that she must follow the direction in which her soul was drawing her, wherever it might lead.

And the more she pondered this "beckoning", the more she realized that it was drawing her to the other side of the river.

The river was wide. It was deep. It was turbulent. You couldn't wade across it. You couldn't swim across it. There was no bridge across it. Yet everything in her heart convinced her that she must cross it, that whatever it was that her heart most desired lay on the other side.

The day dawned when she went down to the water's edge, and put her mind to the problem of how to cross. As she stood there, a young man came up beside her. In his arms he carried a big stone, and he set it down in the river at her feet, inviting her to use it as a stepping stone. Trusting him entirely, she did so. And there she stood all day, perched on her stepping stone. The next day he came again, and the next, and the next, each time bringing another stepping stone, until, after a while, she had already walked halfway out into the river.

Then one morning he didn't come. With a rising sense of panic, she looked round to see what had happened to him. He was a bit late that morning, and it was then that she saw, for the first time, where he was getting the stepping stones.

He was systematically deconstructing her cosy little cottage on the riverbank to create the means for her to cross the river.

To embrace her future, she realized, she must relinquish the securities of her past. And yet the past that she had so cherished was essential to the making of the pathway to the future. And so it happened that when she had come to terms with her loss, she was able to allow it to become the gateway to new possibility.

Margaret Silf

The journey home

There was once a little boy of six years old whose parents died suddenly in an accident. He was taken to live with an aunt who lived a long way away. It was a hard and frightening journey to reach her home. She hadn't been able to fetch the child herself, so she had sent her servant, a rather grim and taciturn man, and the boy was terrified and tearful as together they rode into the dark night. The boy hardly dared to speak, but eventually he plucked up the courage to ask the servant, "Will she still be awake when we arrive?"

"Oh yes," the servant answered, "she'll stay up for you. Soon you will see the light shining in her window."

And, sure enough, soon they reached the clearing and saw the light shining brightly. And the boy's aunt was waiting for him. She lifted him up and held him in her arms and welcomed him into his new home. They had supper by the fire, and then she tucked him up in his new bed and he slept peacefully.

The years passed and the aunt cared for the boy lovingly, as if he were her own. When he grew up he had to leave home and make his way in the world, but one day he learned that his aunt was very ill, and not expected to live much longer. He rushed to her bedside, and found her very weak, and very, very afraid of the death that awaited her.

He took her in his arms and told her the story of how, as a six-year-old boy, he had made that terrifying journey with the taciturn servant, so afraid of all that lay ahead, and how he had watched for the light in her window, and been welcomed so warmly by her into his new home.

"You are about to make a journey just like that," he told her gently. "And you can trust that soon you too will see the lighted windows of heaven, where God will embrace you as you arrive, and that, though the journey may seem long and frightening, it will bring you safely to your new and eternal home."

And his aunt slept peacefully, dreaming of a window where the light was always burning, while her grieving nephew kept a vigil at her bedside.

Retelling of a Russian story by Arthur Gordon

The new lake

It was springtime on the mountain. The fresh spring flowers were just beginning to sprout and show their colours. The birds were gathering building material for their nests. But all was not joy and happiness on the mountain. Over the wintertime there had been landslides, and the terrain had changed. In one place there was a cavernous hole where a rockslide had dislodged a group of large boulders. Nothing was growing in this empty hollow. An air of sadness and failure filled it. It felt like nothing.

But one day the spring rains came. The streams and rivers ran high. The birds took shelter wherever they could find it. But the hole in the mountain could do nothing to protect herself. The water coursed down the mountainside and the rain flooded. She could do nothing but let it all happen.

But when the rains abated, and the summer sun broke through, the flowers gasped. There in their midst was a beautiful mountain lake where the bare hole had been. And the birds swooped down to drink deeply from her fresh waters. And fish took up residence in her clear pools. And the sun made her waters sparkle and painted a reflection of the mountain peaks in her depths. The lake was overjoyed at her transformation.

And, as summer progressed, people came to the valley to admire the new lake and to hike in the mountains. And among them was a hiker who was feeling rather like the lake had felt when she was just a bare hole where nothing grew. When he reached the lake he stopped for a very long time, gazing into her depths.

"This lake is here because the waters found an empty space where they could gather," he thought to himself. "Last year she was just a hole in the ground. Now she is brimming over with life and joy. Could it be so for a human heart, I wonder? Could the flow of transforming grace seek out the empty spaces in *my* life? Could the deep dark hollow of my loss and disappointment become the very space where new life finds entry?"

And the hiker went on his way with a new possibility in his heart and a lighter spring to his step.

Margaret Silf

The sheep who were afraid of the shepherd

Once upon a time on a hillside in a faraway land there was a little black lamb called Laurie. When Laurie was born his parents were very happy indeed, even though his twin was a pure white lamb, who looked the same as most of the other lambs in the flock. Laurie was different, but this only made his parents love him more.

As Laurie grew up, he met other lambs. A few, like him, were black. Most were a greyish colour. Some were white. None of the lambs even noticed what colour they were until one day the shepherd came to check on them. As the shepherd made his inspection, he had nothing but praise for the white lambs. He was rather less kind to the grey lambs. When he came to a black lamb he scolded it, and told it to get itself cleaned up. Gradually the lambs who were not pure white began to think of themselves as unacceptable, not part of the true flock.

Time passed, the lambs grew into sheep, and every time the shepherd came along the not-so-white sheep started to tremble. What if the shepherd were to cast them out of the flock? And every time he came, he scolded them all the more for their alleged imperfections and threatened to send them away.

Inevitably, many of the sheep in the flock began to be afraid of the shepherd. They were afraid that they were not wearing the right kind of fleece. They were afraid of failing to keep in step when he herded them across the hillside. They were afraid to bleat in case the shepherd accused them of insubordination.

Then, one day, a young hiker came by, and stopped to admire the flock. "How beautiful you all are," he said. "But why do you hide behind the bushes? Why are you trembling?"

"We are afraid," said one bold sheep.

"Afraid of what?" asked the young man.

"Afraid of the shepherd. Afraid he will scold us, and cast us from the flock."

The young man scratched his head, puzzled by this revelation.

"It seems to me", he said eventually, "that if you are afraid of the shepherd, that can mean only one thing."

"What's that?" asked the adventurous and curious sheep.

"It can mean only that the shepherd is actually a wolf."

Margaret Silf

The other side of terror

Oftentimes in the summer heat the land would be visited by terrible forest fires. When this happened the people would flee with their animals, terrified of the flames.

One year a great fire came upon the land again, and the people of the tribe were fleeing, desperately trying to outrun the flames. But the fire was rapidly catching up with them, and there was no hope of escape.

Until the wise woman of the tribe suddenly stopped running and addressed the people: "We can never outrun the flames," she told them. "We must turn to face the fire, and run back *through* the flames, to safety on the other side."

Now of course the people shrank in fear at the thought of running back through the flames, but they respected the wise woman and heeded her advice. First they drenched their children with the remaining water they were carrying. Any surplus water they used to drench their animals and themselves as best they could. Then, holding their children close in their arms, they ran back through the flames.

Some died. But most came through to safety beyond the flames. All were scarred and became known as "the people with burn scars on their skin". They had faced their worst fears, and broken through to the life that beckons on the other side of terror.

Retelling of a traditional Lakota story

The rescue dime

Sister Maureen had entered the convent when she was only eighteen. She would never forget that day – how she had said goodbye to her family, not knowing when she would see them again, the tears in her mother's eyes, bravely held back, her father's forced cheerfulness, the view from the back of the bus as her home village became smaller and smaller in the distance, until it disappeared altogether.

As the bus gathered speed, carrying her into a future she couldn't begin to imagine, her heart contracted in her chest, and her fingers curled around a single dime she was keeping in her pocket. A single dime. It was all she had, but it would be enough to make a phone call home if the worst came to the worst. It was the last connection, the safety line that would, if she really needed it, bring her parents hurrying to fetch her and take her back to all that was trusted and familiar. It was her rescue dime.

Many years passed. Maureen grew older and became a respected senior sister in the convent. She taught in school, and became head teacher. The children loved her, and she them. When thoughts of home rose up in her mind, she would still, every so often, remember the rescue dime, and now she would smile as she recalled her youthful anxieties. Eventually she forgot the rescue dime. It had served its purpose. She didn't need it any more.

The time came for Sister Maureen to retire from teaching. It was her last day at school. There was a knock at her door and a little girl came in. Maureen knew her well. A year earlier she had arrived at the school, a tiny refugee from a war-torn African country, adopted into an American family. Maureen remembered how she had comforted this frightened, homesick child and guided her gently through this huge transition in her young life. Now, on her own last day in school, she greeted the little girl warmly.

The child clutched an envelope in her small hand. "This is for you, Sister," she said in her still faltering English, and turned to leave, but then changed her mind and ran back to give Maureen a big hug.

As the door closed behind her, Maureen opened the envelope. Inside was a card the child had made herself, with a message: "Thank you for looking after me. I love you. Please use this to help the sisters." And there beneath the words, carefully taped to the card, was a shiny new dime.

Margaret Silf

The truck driver

There was once a long-distance truck driver who had been newly recruited by a haulage company transporting goods across Canada.

He reported for his first night. His task was to drive the truck across the whole of Canada, from Montreal to Vancouver. It would take five days and he would be driving mainly by night. He was given the keys to the truck, and he climbed in and switched on the engine.

The headlights came on. He gazed for a few moments into the black of the night beyond the reach of their beams.

"How foolish is this?" he said to himself. "I am embarking on a journey of over four thousand kilometres, and my light only reaches for just a few metres into the darkness."

Perhaps the fledgling truck driver lost his nerve at this point, switched off the engine, and went home.

Or perhaps he began to drive. If so, he would have discovered that the light always travelled with him.

Margaret Silf

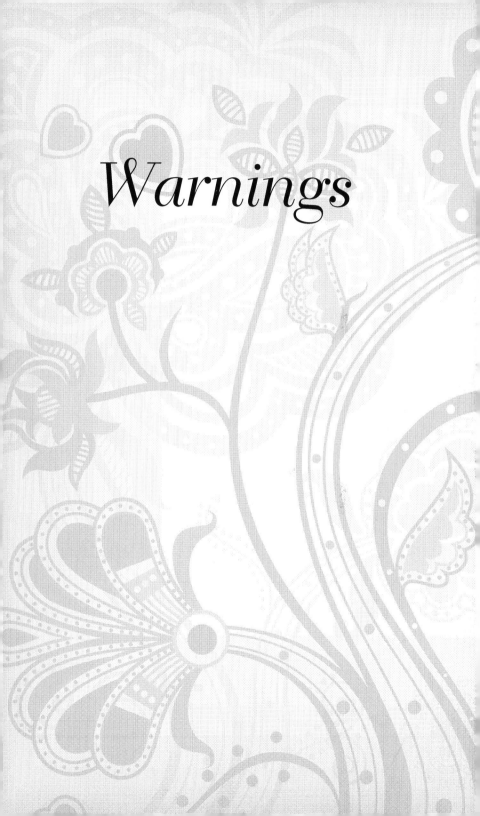

Warnings

A fish out of water

Once there was a beautiful tropical fish pond in the garden of a house set in the midst of the Malaysian rainforest.

Every morning the people who lived in the house would watch the fish swimming round in circles. One day one of these beautiful fish was heard to say to the others, "We can never be free here in this pool, with nothing but water all around us. I'm getting out. The water is nothing but an illusion."

The others took no notice of him. He had always been a bit of a rebel, and always thought he was cleverer than all the fish elders who had gone before.

Nevertheless, one morning he made his bid for freedom. That morning the people who came to the pool saw a big fish leap out of the water onto a rocky shelf. There he flopped and flailed around for some time, gasping and choking and trying to declare his independence and prove that no one needs the water.

And finally, just as he was about to expire, he flopped back into the water. It was his moment of enlightenment. When he had recovered, he told all the other fish, "The water is everything. It is the only reality we have. It is the mystery in which we live and move and have our being."

The other fish took no notice. They all knew the truth about the water, but every fish has to discover it for himself.

Margaret Silf

A little piece of truth

One day the devil was out for a walk with a friend. As they wandered the ways of the earth, they noticed someone walking ahead of them. Eventually the man stopped and bent down to pick something up.

"What has he found?" the friend asked the devil.

"Oh, he's just found a little piece of truth lying in the grass," the devil replied nonchalantly.

"Doesn't that worry you?" his friend continued.

"Not at all," the devil replied with a contented smile. "I'll just let him make a belief system out of it."

Retelling of a story by Anthony de Mello

Beg, borrow or steal

One dark night a thief made his way through the streets of an affluent suburb of the city. In his sack he had a cache of jewellery – a couple of diamond rings, some pearl earrings, a gold bracelet, two or three expensive watches, and a collection of valuable silver coins. But one thing concerned him. He lived in a hostel with others, and there was no privacy. Where would he hide his ill-gotten gains so that no one would find them, and where could he keep them until it was safe to sell them?

Then he had an idea. He asked the owner of the all-night takeaway for a plastic carrier bag, put the stolen goods in the bag, tied a tight knot around it with strong cord, and placed it very carefully in the river, lodged under a big stone, and in a place he had mentally noted, so that he could return to it when enough time had passed and the hue and cry had died down.

Time passed. Meanwhile, the beavers who lived in the river were building their lodge for the winter. Imagine their delight when they found this unexpected treasure hanging right there in the water, as though it had been deposited there especially for their use. They rapidly incorporated the jewels into their construction. When the thief came back for his booty, all he could find was the chewed-up remains of the plastic bag.

But there instead was the most expensively decorated penthouse in town – a bejewelled dam carefully built across the water – and the beavers enjoyed their winter in splendour.

Margaret Silf

Co-dependency

Once upon a time there was a very pretty little bird, with beautifully coloured feathers. She flew around the forest every day, happily searching for a worm to eat for supper.

In the forest there also lived a sly fox. He watched the pretty little bird day after day, and one day he approached her with an offer.

"Little bird, you use up all your energy each day searching for worms to eat. I could easily bring you a fresh worm each day, and you could save your energy for other things. All I would ask in return is that each time I bring you a worm, you give me just one little feather."

The bird pondered this offer, and eventually she agreed to the meal deal.

And, true to his word, the fox brought her a fresh worm every day, and every day she gave him one of her pretty feathers in return. This arrangement continued for many weeks. The little bird had given away all her breast feathers, and now she was sacrificing her wings in return for her daily worm.

Then one day she had come to the last of her wing feathers. That day the fox presented her with her very last worm. She gave him her very last feather so that she could no longer fly. And the fox enjoyed a very tasty supper that night as he ate her up.

Source unknown

Confrontation

A US naval warship was once under way, close to a rather hazardous coastline. An approaching presence was noted on the ship's radar, so the commander of the vessel sent out a message:

"USS IRRESISTIBLE FORCE to unidentified oncoming vessel: We are on a collision course. Suggest you adjust your course 10 deg NW."

The response came instantly:

"LHS IMMOVABLE OBJECT to USS IRRESISTIBLE FORCE: Suggest YOU adjust *your* course."

And then:

"USS IRRESISTIBLE FORCE to LHS IMMOVABLE OBJECT: This is a vessel of the US Navy. Adjust your course immediately. Collision imminent."

And again the response:

"LHS IMMOVABLE OBJECT to USS IRRESISTIBLE FORCE: Suggest YOU adjust *your* course."

Finally, in exasperation:

"USS IRRESISTIBLE FORCE to LHS IMMOVABLE OBJECT: I am the commander of this US naval battleship, and I COMMAND you to adjust your course immediately."

To which came the response:

"LHS IMMOVABLE OBJECT to USS IRRESISTIBLE FORCE: Repeat: I most strongly urge you to adjust *your* course. I am a lighthouse!"

Source unknown

Follow the goat

There was once an old patriarch who led a nomadic life, along with his people and their herds of sheep and goats. The old patriarch had many children, among them a favourite son who cared for the goats. And among the goats this son had a special favourite, whom he loved dearly. This goat was black and white with long, floppy ears.

The boy loved to play with this goat, but the goat had a mind of its own and was forever scampering away, getting lost in rocky crevices, and the boy would go searching for him. The father was very anxious, lest the boy should come to harm while going after the goat.

One day the tribe broke camp and set out for new pastures. To the father's dismay, the boy was nowhere to be found. For three whole days he searched in vain for his son. On the third day he heard the bleating of the goat, but could see no sign of the boy.

Furious that the goat had led the boy to his death, the patriarch took out his dagger and slit the goat's throat in his rage. And as the goat lay dying, one long floppy ear fell forward. Inside the goat's ear was a tiny scroll, on which the boy had written a note: "Father, I followed the goat to a cave high in the hills. On the other side of the cave I found the promised land that we have all been looking for. I will stay here and await your arrival with all our people. The goat knows the way. Follow the goat!"

Retelling of a story by William J. Bausch

How to catch a monkey

If you ever need to catch a monkey there is a simple method. Just place a piece of tantalizing fruit inside a cage. Then wait until the monkey comes by. Watch as it puts its paw through the bars of the cage, and grasps the fruit.

You can be sure that you have got your monkey. He will not let go of that fruit, even though it costs him his freedom. All he needs to do to be free is to let go of his fruit. But what we cling to robs us of our freedom.

What a blessing that we are not monkeys!

Margaret Silf

The devil in disguise

Once upon a time the devil was determined to get into heaven.

To achieve this, he disguised himself as Jesus. That way, he felt sure, no one would dare to refuse him access to heaven. That would be unthinkable.

Now it happened that on the day in question St Peter was away on heavenly business and St Thomas had been left in charge of immigration. St Thomas, you will remember, was the disciple who doubted Jesus' resurrection, and insisted on seeing Jesus' wounds before he would be convinced.

Well, things were quiet at check-in when the devil appeared, looking for all the world like the risen Jesus.

Thomas duly stopped him at the pearly gates and after a few minutes of careful consideration he refused him entry.

When the other disciples heard what had happened they were horrified. "How could you have refused to let Jesus into heaven?" they demanded.

"That wasn't Jesus," he replied with calm conviction. "It was the devil."

"But it looked exactly like Jesus," they retorted. "How could you be so sure?"

"The devil has no wounds," said Thomas quietly.

Margaret Silf

Distraction

A poor peasant was surprised to hear the clip-clop of a horseman approaching as he was walking along the path. When the horseman saw him, he pulled up his reins and stopped the horse, to have a friendly conversation with the peasant.

The peasant, even more surprised at this gesture, admired the horse effusively. The longing in his eyes was obvious, and the horseman's heart was moved.

"Would you like to own a horse like this?" he asked him.

The peasant's eyes nearly popped out of his head. "Sir, there is nothing I would love more than to own a horse like this," he replied.

"Tell you what," offered the horseman. "If you can recite the Lord's Prayer without any hesitation or digression or distraction, you can have this horse as a gift."

Hardly able to believe his ears, the peasant immediately began to recite the Lord's Prayer. He got as far as "lead us not into temptation" before he stopped, distracted, and asked: "Do I get the saddle as well?"

And at this the horseman rode away.

Margaret Silf

The fate of the snail

There was once a little snail, who was very happy with his itinerant lifestyle. He crawled contentedly around the world, carrying his home on his back, and when he felt like resting for a while he just stopped and curled up inside his cosy shell.

One day his wanderings brought him to a large estate, and in the middle of this estate was a splendid castle. It took him a long time, of course, to crawl up the walls surrounding the estate and down the other side, and then to make his way through all the landscaped gardens, but eventually he made it to the castle itself. And it has to be said that he enjoyed the journey, stopping to savour every new experience along the way.

And late one evening his travels brought him to the grand entrance to the castle. There, to his surprise, he met another creature – a tall being dressed in fine clothes and walking on two legs. A being without a house on his back. A human being.

"Good evening, little snail," said the human being, bending low to examine his adventurous little guest. "And how are you today?"

"I'm very well," replied the snail. "But I am so impressed by your magnificent castle. I wish I could have a castle like yours, instead of this very humble little home of mine."

"Well, little snail," said the human being, "I am actually something of a wizard, and if this is really your wish, I could turn your snail shell into a splendid castle and you could live as magnificently as I do. But you must be very sure first that this is what you truly desire."

"Oh, it is, it is!" cried the snail, almost toppling over himself with excitement.

And so the wizard said the magic words, and slowly the snail's shell began to get heavier and heavier, and eventually it turned into a magnificent castle.

Gradually the wizard got used to his new neighbour. One morning he walked past the snail's castle and greeted him with a bright "Good morning, little snail. How are you today?"

But all that he heard by way of reply was a tiny muffled sob from the middle of the snail's castle.

"I'm so unhappy," said the squeaky little voice. "I have this wonderful castle, but it completely prevents me from moving anywhere. I am a prisoner here. Can't you let me out again, please? I long to keep on exploring the world as I used to."

But it is impossible to turn back time. There was to be no rescue for the snail, trapped in his castle. The wizard could not reverse the spell. Thousands of years later scientists came to explore the region, and there they found a perfectly formed fossil of a creature that had once lived – and moved – in these parts.

"See," they told each other, "this must be where civilization first began, when living creatures gave up their freedom to roam, and settled instead in one place and started to acquire more and more possessions. See how this simple home has evolved into an elaborate castle, and see how it has buried the creature that once lived here. These must have been the creatures that chose wealth over freedom, and now they are forever fossils."

Margaret Silf

155

The fruit tree

There was once a beautiful garden. In the middle of the garden was a magnificent fruit tree, its branches weighed down with every kind of fruit you could imagine. And in the garden lived a tribe of people who all enjoyed the fruit that grew on the tree.

At first it was easy to live like this. Everyone plucked the fruit from the lower branches and all were satisfied. But with the passing of time the lower branches were stripped bare, with only sparse amounts of fruit growing to replace what had been eaten.

Still, there was plenty of fruit on the higher branches, so the taller people of the tribe could reach the higher fruit, but the shorter people had to go without, unless some of the taller people took pity on them and were willing to share.

More time passed, and before long the middle branches of the tree were also stripped bare, and even the taller people couldn't reach the fruit. But necessity is the mother of invention, and so it happened that a few of the tallest people invented a ladder. With the help of this new technology they could reach the fruit at the top of the tree. But the people who didn't have access to the ladder then also had to go without the fruit, unless any of the people on the ladder took pity and were willing to share.

And then one day there came a great storm. The tree shook. The people on the ladder quailed with fear lest they should fall, and they clung to the topmost branches like monkeys. And the wind blew, and the remaining fruit came plunging down to earth. And the small people, who had lived so long on so little, immediately knew what to do. They picked up the fallen fruit, gave thanks to the great spirit of life, ate the fruit, planted the seeds, and grew a new orchard.

Margaret Silf

83

The guru's cat

There was once a famous guru who lived in an ashram in India. This guru was so wise that many people came each day to sit at his feet and listen to his teaching.

These gatherings were often disturbed, however, by the habit of the ashram cat, who liked to wander around among the disciples, and became a distraction.

To solve this problem, the guru decided to tie the cat to a tree while he was teaching, so that it could no longer distract the people.

Eventually the guru died, but the people continued the practice of tying the cat to a tree during their daily gatherings.

Finally, the cat itself died. And the people acquired a new cat, which they duly tied to the tree every day. This became the way things were done in the ashram. Whenever there was a time of teaching or worship, a cat must be tied to a tree.

Today, many generations later, learned disciples of that guru's teaching write obscure treatises on the liturgical and theological significance of the cat to the practice of worship, and on the correct choice of the tree to which it must be tied. In fact, many people have completely forgotten the guru. But everyone knows about the importance of the cat.

Retelling of a story by Anthony de Mello

The king's bed

There was once a terrible tyrant who believed that everything and everyone in the world should fit in with what he thought was the right way to do things.

He had a guest suite in his palace, where he entertained visitors, and one day he called his carpenters together and instructed them to make a bed for the guest room.

"How long shall the bed be, your majesty?" they asked.

"Exactly five feet," he said. "My height exactly."

Now, because he was a terrible tyrant, everyone was afraid of him, and no one dared to suggest that not every guest would be the same height as the king. It would have meant certain death to question the king's instructions, even though it was obvious that many guests would not be able to fit into such a short bed.

And so the bed was made – exactly five feet long. Then the king instructed that whenever a guest came, if he didn't fit the bed, he must be cut down to size if he was too tall, or stretched on the rack if he was too short.

Many guests came. Some survived the bed, because they were five feet tall exactly. Many more found, at bedtime, that they couldn't fit the bed, and so the king's servants came along and cut off their feet or their heads, until they were made to fit.

No one would be so foolish or so tyrannical today, as to try to force everyone to fit their own mould. No one would be so arrogant as to assume that they alone knew the right way of doing things. No one today would instil such fear in their servants that no one would dare to raise a dissenting voice.

Or would they?

Retelling of an Ancient Greek legend

The king's treasure

There was once a king who went to war, and came home after the campaign with a large chest of precious jewels he had gained.

When he got home he stowed his jewels away in a room in the castle. But he soon found that he couldn't sleep at night. He lay awake worrying that someone might break in and steal his treasure.

"I must build up the defences around my castle," he thought to himself. "I must put a stronger lock on the door. But how will I pay the locksmith?"

And the answer seemed obvious. He would sell one of his precious jewels to raise the money to pay for a stronger lock.

But still he worried. Actually the whole door was rather weak. Thieves could easily force it open in spite of the new lock. He would have to have a stronger door. But how would he pay the carpenter?

So once again he sold off some of the jewels, in order to pay the carpenter, and the new door was duly installed.

But this brought the king no peace. He needed altogether stronger walls. And so more jewels were sold in order to pay the builders to fortify the castle walls.

But still he found no peace. Actually the whole castle needed to be surrounded by a high wall. And yet more jewels were sold off to pay the stonemasons to build a high wall all the way round the castle.

But still he could not sleep easy in his bed, and so the king decided he needed a moat around the castle. It would cost a lot to make a moat. A whole team of people came to work on it, digging out the trench, strengthening the sides, connecting the moat to the water supply. It took a year to make the moat and cost the king so much that he had to sell off the last of the precious jewels in his chest to pay for it.

And finally the king was at peace, knowing that at last he was adequately defended. Unfortunately, as a result, he had nothing left to defend.

Margaret Silf

Life Lessons

The sun and the north wind

It seemed like forever that the sun and the north wind had been arguing with each other about which of them was stronger.

One day they noticed a man walking along the road, wearing a thick winter coat.

"You see that man down there," said the north wind to the sun. "Now you will see how strong I am. I will blow that man's coat right off his shoulders."

And with this the wind blew, and blew, and blew. But far from blowing the man's coat away, all that the wind achieved was to make the man pull the coat even more firmly around himself and keep on walking, head bent against the wind.

"Now it's my turn," said the sun. "You have shown that you are not strong enough to blow away his coat. Now let me try."

And the sun came out and shone down warmly on the man, and within a very short time he stopped, took off his coat, laid it over his arm, and kept on walking.

"Gentleness and warmth", said the sun with a smile, "can often achieve more than force and coercion." And the north wind subsided, and went back to the hills to think things over.

Retelling of a traditional fable

Donkey in the well

A farmer had a donkey. The donkey was old and rather unsteady on its legs, and one day it fell into an old disused well.

The farmer searched for the donkey and eventually heard it braying from the bottom of the well.

When the farmer asked his neighbours to help him get his donkey out of the well, they all laughed at him. "What? Rescue that old donkey?" they scorned. "He's neither use nor ornament. He was stupid enough to fall down the well, so why bother getting him out? You should just throw earth down there and bury him, and put him out of his misery."

The farmer was dismayed, but on his own he was quite unable to get the donkey out of the well. So very unhappily he had to agree to his neighbours' plan. They began to throw clumps of earth down the old well to bury the donkey.

At first the distressed braying continued, but eventually it grew less and less, until it stopped completely. And the neighbours continued to throw earth down the shaft of the well.

But the donkey was not going to give up so easily. Every time a load of earth descended on him he kicked it off and stepped on top of it, gradually working his way to the top of the well.

Imagine the farmer's surprise, therefore, when the donkey finally emerged, head held high, and stepped out of the top of the well. The farmer was so pleased to have his old donkey back. He threw his arms round the donkey's neck. And perhaps we can believe his story that, as he did so, he heard the donkey say these words: "When life throws dirt at you, use it to rise above it."

Source unknown

Nature versus nurture

A group of tourists from a rich Western country were enjoying their stay in a safari park in South Africa. They were star-struck by all the exotic animals they had seen, and spent much time speaking of the wonders of nature, and how awesome creation is, as they sipped their sundowners beside the pool at the safari lodge.

Night fell, and the bush took on a life of its own. Safe in their lodge they dreamed of the paradise they had discovered and their plans for the next day. And early the next morning some of them rose to greet the sunrise and to enjoy a swim in the pool.

They were more than a little surprised to see that the surrounding bush had been trampled overnight and that elephants had visited their lodge while they slept, and drunk the swimming pool dry.

Margaret Silf

89

The deaf frog

Once upon a time there was a bunch of small frogs who arranged a running competition. The goal was to reach the top of a very high tower. A big crowd had gathered around the tower to see the race and to cheer on the contestants... The race began...

No one in the crowd really believed that the little frogs would reach the top of the tower.

You heard statements such as:

"Oh, way too difficult!!"

"They will *never* make it to the top."

"Not a chance that they will succeed. The tower is too high!"

The little frogs began collapsing. One by one... Except for those who, in a fresh tempo, were climbing higher and higher...The crowd continued to yell, "It is too difficult!!! No one will make it!"

More little frogs got tired and gave up...

But one continued higher and higher and higher...

This one wouldn't give up.

By the end, all the others had given up climbing the tower. Except for the one little frog who, after a big effort, was the only one who reached the top!

Then all the other little frogs naturally wanted to know how this one frog had managed to do it.

A contestant asked the little frog how he had found the strength to succeed and reach the goal.

It turned out...

... that the winner was *deaf!*

Source unknown

The fairy shoemaker

Michael was one of thirteen children. They were a very poor family, but he had heard that the leprechauns kept a pot of gold buried somewhere in the forest, and that the location of the hoard was close to where they did their shoemaking work.

So imagine Michael's joy one day when he was playing in the forest and he heard the sound of "tap, tap, tap".

"That has to be the leprechaun shoemaker," he thought to himself. "But I mustn't disturb him, because he will put a curse on me if I do."

So Michael waited until nightfall to go back to the spot where he had heard the shoemaker at work. He had marked the tree nearest to the spot with a cross so that he could find it again. The moon came up, and the stars came out, and Michael set off into the forest, convinced that now the fairy shoemaker would be in bed fast asleep.

Imagine his dismay, therefore, when he reached the spot and looked for the tree he had marked, to discover that every single tree in that part of the forest was marked with a cross.

Michael was bitterly disappointed. He had so wanted to bring back the pot of gold to help his parents feed the family. It was almost enough to make him stop believing in fairies.

Weeks passed, and then strange new things began to stir in the village. A new lumber yard was opened, and many people, including Michael's older brothers, found jobs, helping to fell the trees that had been marked with a cross. The land where the trees had been was allocated to the villagers for smallholdings, and Michael's family were able to have a cow, some pigs, and some chickens, so there was now plenty of food for them all.

But in all of this development, a small copse of trees was left standing, for the fairies. Everyone knew that it was a fairy place, and treated it with great respect. But Michael knew more than this. He knew it was the spot where the fairy shoemaker worked, and that the leprechauns had given the village a pot of gold in their own special way. He often went back there to say thank you to the leprechauns. And always, when he visited, the woodpecker high in the fairy trees would keep up his "tap, tap, tap, tap".

Margaret Silf

The fence and the waterhole

The journey seemed endless as Bruce and his guest drove round the ranch. Ranches in Australia can be as big as a whole country in Europe. The cattle were roaming freely in all directions.

"How do you make sure your cattle stay on your own ranch?" the guest asked. "How do you keep them fenced in?"

"Can you imagine trying to erect a fence around an area of land this size?" Bruce replied.

"Of course not," his guest thought. "Impossible."

"No," said Bruce. "It's not about fences. That would never work. It's about waterholes. The cattle stay close to where they find water. The way we keep them home is by attracting them, not coercing them. Cattle are like people. Fence them in, and they will rebel. Offer them what they want and need, and they will draw closer."

Retelling of an Australian wisdom story

The money carousel

A customer was doing some business at the bank one day. When she had finished, the bank manager asked her, "Is there anything else I can do for you today?"

She thought for a moment and then said, "Yes, actually. There is a question I have, though I don't know whether you can help me with it."

"Try me," invited the bank manager.

"Well," said the customer. "I read in the newspapers of the vast sums that, it seems, almost every country in the world owes in the way of national debt. Can you perhaps tell me: Who do we owe it all to?"

The bank manager scratched his head. "I have no idea," he admitted. "I think maybe we all owe it to each other."

And then he went on to tell her this story:

Once upon a time a traveller arrived at a small town in the Wild West. When he arrived he was unsure whether he wanted to stay overnight in the town, and decided to have a look around before making a decision. So he went to the innkeeper and gave him $100, asking him to reserve a room for him in case he decided to stay the night, and promising to come back in the evening and either stay the night or take back his deposit.

The innkeeper readily agreed. He went straight round to the butcher, and used the $100 to pay off the money he owed him. The butcher then went to the grocer and paid off the money he owed her. The grocer in turn went to the brewer and paid him what she owed him. The brewer then went to the innkeeper to pay off the debt he had accumulated with him.

At night the traveller returned, having decided not to stay overnight in this one-horse town. He took back his $100 and moved on.

The bank manager smiled. "It's a crazy merry-go-round we are all riding on, I guess. But the banks know how to ride it. They charge interest every time they lend the $100, so at the end of the day they are the only winners of the carousel race."

And the customer withdrew her money from the bank and put it in a teapot under the bed.

Margaret Silf

The monkey's gift

Once upon a time a traveller was walking in the bush when, out of sheer malice, a monkey sitting on a high tree branch threw a coconut at him.

The man rubbed his bruised head, and then stopped to pick up the coconut. First he drank the milk. Then he ate the tender flesh of the coconut. And then he sat down in a shady spot and patiently carved a bowl out of the coconut shell.

And finally he looked up to the treetop and thanked the monkey, and went on his way.

Retelling of a traditional African tale

The smuggler's secret

There was once a smuggler who was constantly crossing the border between Persia and Greece. Every week he would arrive at the crossing point with his two donkeys each loaded with a large bale of straw.

The customs officials were, naturally, suspicious of all this activity, and every time he arrived at the border checkpoint they searched assiduously through the straw, determined to find the goods he was obviously smuggling into the country. But all their efforts were in vain: they could never find any contraband, and they had to let him pass.

Meanwhile the man became richer and richer, until at last he was able to retire into comfortable old age. One day one of the former customs officers, now also retired and getting very old, met him and they sat down together for a drink, to talk about old times.

"Tell me," the former customs man asked, "now that we are both old men and not far from the end of our lives, and you can tell me the truth without fear of punishment. You used to cross the border every week with your bales of hay, and we always suspected you but we could never find anything in all that straw. Tell me now, just for old times' sake, what were you up to in those days? What was it that you were smuggling across the border all those years ago?"

"Donkeys," replied the retired smuggler with a wry smile.

Retelling of a Sufi story

The tailor's button

Once upon a time there was a tailor who made clothes for everyone in the town but never made clothes for himself. Instead, he practised "make do and mend", and gave the money he saved by not wasting anything to the poor people of the town.

One day he noticed that his overcoat was fraying at the edges, so he cut it down and made a short jacket.

Then one day he saw that the jacket had a rip in the sleeve, so he cut it down to make a waistcoat.

Then one day he found a hole in the pocket of the waistcoat, so he cut it down to make a scarf.

Then one day he noticed that the scarf was getting frayed and had holes in it, so he cut it down to make a necktie.

Then one day he noticed that the necktie was getting badly stained, so he cut it down to make a handkerchief.

Then one day he noticed that the handkerchief was getting too thin to use, so he cut it down and made a button.

And one day... he lost the button!

Now it happened that soon afterwards the angels were sweeping the floors of heaven and they found the tailor's button. They brought it to God, because it really was very beautiful. God, in turn, kept it in a place very close to his heart because he loved the tailor with his frugal ways and compassionate heart.

Eventually the good tailor died and found himself standing at heaven's gate, lost and rather frightened, and dressed in rags. And God came to greet him, holding out the button in recognition. "Welcome to your eternal home," said God. "We have been looking forward to your coming. We have something that belongs to you. This button is worth its weight in gold because it was made by one who has a heart of gold."

Source unknown

Two wolves

An old grandfather used to tell his grandson bedtime stories, and the boy's favourite story was this:

"In every human heart two wolves live," he told the child. "These two wolves live in our hearts until the day we die, and they are constantly in conflict with each other until then."

"What are these wolves like, who live in our hearts," asked the boy, "and why do they fight each other all the time?"

"One wolf is about all the things we value in ourselves and each other," explained Grandfather. "Things like generosity and compassion and tolerance. The other wolf is about the things we wish were not there, like resentment and bitterness and envy."

"So, Grandfather," asked the boy. "Which wolf wins?"

Grandfather was silent for a moment and then replied, "The one that you feed."

Retelling of a Native American story

Three bottles of wine

There was once a wealthy man who had an important position in the corporate world, and had three sons. One day a customer gave the man a gift of three bottles of wine. Not just any bottles, but three bottles of very expensive wine. Each bottle had a value of $2,000.

The man decided that he would give one of these bottles of wine to each of his three sons. He placed no conditions on the gift, but he was interested to see what each son would do with it.

The youngest son held a big party, inviting all his friends to come, to eat, drink, and be merry, and giving each of the guests just one small sip of the expensive wine, just for the experience.

The next son, who was soon to be married, immediately sold his bottle of wine and put the $2,000 in the bank.

The eldest son, who was married with a young family, and whose hobby was woodcarving, thought very carefully about what he would do with the bottle of wine. He didn't decide for quite a long time, trusting that he would know what to do when the right solution revealed itself. One day he saw an advertisement in the newspaper for timber for sale. He went along to the loggers' camp, and there he was offered a large, solid tree trunk of fine northern white cedar. So he came to an arrangement with the logger to exchange his bottle of wine for this tree trunk.

When he got home he told the family of his decision. He went with his four children to the logging camp and they dragged the tree trunk back to their own garden. Then he taught them how to chisel and plane it, shape it into planks, and use it to create a canoe, big enough for the whole family to fit in. The project took them several years, and gave them great satisfaction as they worked on it together, but for many more years after the canoe was finished, indeed until the children were long grown and had children of their own, that family enjoyed endless happy weekends and holidays together, exploring the lakes and rivers of their country.

And when Grandfather came to stay, he too enjoyed a trip in the canoe his son and grandchildren had built, and marvelled that an extravagant gift had been turned into a lifetime of joy and adventure.

Margaret Silf

Things will change

Once a man fell upon really hard times. First he lost his job, and could no longer keep up the payments on his home. Then his wife left him and took the children with her, and he fell into deep despair.

Then one day he heard tell of a very wise sage who lived far away, over the ocean, over the mountains, in India. He decided to seek out this wise one and ask for his counsel.

And so he journeyed far across the sea, over the mountains, up and down the river valleys, until after a very, very long time he arrived at the dwelling of the wise sage, and told him the sorry story. The sage listened carefully, and when the story was told he looked deep into the eyes of his visitor and pronounced his wisdom: "Things will change," he assured him.

Feeling very dissatisfied by this vague, unhelpful answer, the man went all the way back home, up and down the valleys, over the mountains, and across the sea.

Time passed, and the wind of fortune changed direction. The man found a job. He saved enough money to get his house back. His wife returned with the children. They were happy again. He remembered the sage's words to him. "Surely, he was absolutely right," he marvelled. "I must go and tell him how right he was. I must go and thank him."

And so he set out for a second time, across the ocean, over the mountains, up and down the valleys, until he reached the dwelling of the wise sage. Delighted at his renewed fortune he recounted how the sage had been completely right, and everything had indeed changed for the better. The sage listened carefully, looked deep into the eyes of his visitor, and pronounced his wisdom once more: "Things will change."

Source unknown

Whose problem?

A man who worked in the City of London used to take the train into work every morning, and met up with a colleague who boarded the train at the same suburban station.

On arrival at the London terminus the two friends walked the short distance to their City office, and on the way the first man always stopped to buy a newspaper from the same newsagent. This newsagent, however, was a rude and surly man who always had some unpleasant comment to make to his customer as he sold him the newspaper.

One day the man's friend, unable to understand his apparent tolerance of this behaviour, asked him, "Tell me, why do you keep on buying your morning newspaper from that rude and churlish fellow?"

To which his friend replied, "Why should I allow *his* problem to dictate where *I* buy my newspaper?"

Source unknown

Total commitment

One day a hen and a pig were walking along the road together, enjoying the sunny morning and having a friendly conversation. As they turned a corner they noticed a big poster by the roadside. It was an advertisement for the "Great British Breakfast", and it featured such goodies as fried potatoes, tomatoes, mushrooms, and, first and foremost, two fried eggs, a couple of sausages, and a few rashers of sizzling crisp bacon.

"Ah," sighed the hen, "just take a look at that. What a picture! Doesn't it make you feel proud, to be chosen to participate in such a wonderful institution as the great British breakfast?"

"Hmm," replied the pig. "It may be 'participation' for you, but for me it is total commitment."

Participation is free. Commitment will cost you!

Retelling of a British folk tale

Acknowledgments

Wisdom stories live in the atmosphere we breathe. They have a life of their own, and they evolve and change with every retelling. In many cases, it is impossible to identify their origins, and most of the stories in this collection have been gleaned over the years from oral retellings. Whenever the source of a story is known, it is detailed in this Acknowledgments section and referred to briefly beneath the story itself. Every effort has been made to trace and contact copyright owners for material used in this book. We apologize for any inadvertent omissions or errors.

1. Source unknown.
2. Retelling by Margaret Silf of a story from *Keepers of the Story* by Megan McKenna and Tony Cowan, published by Orbis Books, 1997.
3. Story by Margaret Silf.
4. Story by Margaret Silf, inspired by a sermon delivered in 1978 at the University of Keele, Staffordshire, England, by Brian McClorry SJ.
5. Retelling by Margaret Silf of a traditional Jewish story, heard from a Californian storyteller, Sharon Halsey-Hoover, Inscape Ministries, Laguna Woods, California.
6. Story by Margaret Silf.
7. Extract from *Illusions: The Adventures of a Reluctant Messiah* by Richard Bach, published by William Heinemann. Reprinted by permission of The Random House Group Limited.
8. Retelling by Margaret Silf of a story from *Sower's Seeds of Virtue* by Brian Cavanaugh, published by Paulist Press, 1997.

9. Story by Margaret Silf.
10. Source unknown.
11. Excerpt from *Taking Flight* by Anthony de Mello, copyright © 1988 by Gujurat Sahitya Prakash. Used by permission of Doubleday, an imprint of the Knopf Doubleday Publishing Group, a division of Random House LLC. All rights reserved.
12. Story by Margaret Silf.
13. Story by Margaret Silf (the first part of this story is a retelling of a true event; the ending has been added).
14. Source unknown.
15. Retelling by Margaret Silf of a traditional story.
16. Retelling by Margaret Silf of a Sufi story attributed by Idries Shah to the sixteenth-century Balkan Sufi Sayed Jafar of the Gulshani order.
17. Source unknown.
18. Story by Margaret Silf.
19. Retelling by Margaret Silf of a traditional Lakota story.
20. Retelling by Margaret Silf of a story by Brian Campbell SJ, found on the website of Loyola Press, 2012.
21. Story by Margaret Silf.
22. Story generously shared from the personal experience of Mary Robertson, Calgary, Canada.
23. Story by Margaret Silf, inspired by Lake Louise and Moraine Lake, Banff National Park, Alberta, Canada.
24. Source unknown.
25. Retelling by Margaret Silf of a story from *Touching the Heart: Tales for the Human Journey*, by William J. Bausch, Twenty-Third Publications, 2007.
26. Story by Margaret Silf.
27. Retelling by Margaret Silf of an Australian aboriginal story heard in Melbourne
28. Source unknown (heard from Sharon Halsey-Hoover).
29. Retelling by Margaret Silf of a true story, recounted by Yevgeny Yevtushenko in *A Precocious Autobiography*, Dutton, 1963.

30. Story by Margaret Silf, based on a true story from England.
31. Retelling by Margaret Silf of a story heard in Australia, source unknown.
32. Story by Margaret Silf
33. Retelling by Margaret Silf of a traditional story.
34. Story by Margaret Silf.
35. Retelling by Margaret Silf of a story from *Sower's Seeds of Virtue*, Brian Cavanaugh, Paulist Press, 1997.
36. Retelling by Margaret Silf of a Swedish folk story.
37. Story by Margaret Silf, based on a story heard in Hong Kong.
38. Story by Margaret Silf of a true incident encountered in a large port in north-east England.
39. Retelling by Margaret Silf of a story by Sr. Jose Hobday from *Touching the Heart: Tales for the Human Journey*, by William J. Bausch, Twenty-Third Publications, 2007.
40. Retelling by Margaret Silf of a story from *Twelve and One-Half Keys* by Edward Hays, published by Forest of Peace Books, 1981.
41. Retelling by Margaret Silf of a Native American story.
42. Source unknown.
43. Retelling by Margaret Silf of a traditional German folk story.
44. Source unknown.
45. Story by Margaret Silf, loosely based on a story heard in a kindergarten in Massachusetts.
46. Retelling by Margaret Silf of a story from *The Devil's Storybook* by Natalie Babbitt, published by Farrer, Straus & Giroux, 1984.
47. Retelling by Margaret Silf of a traditional story.
48. Story by Margaret Silf, based on a story generously shared by Bishop Barbara Andrews, British Columbia, Canada.
49. Retelling by Margaret Silf of a story from *150 Stories for Preachers and Teachers* by Jack McArdle, published by The Columba Press, 1990.
50. Retelling by Margaret Silf of a story from *Taking Flight* by Anthony de Mello, published by Doubleday New York, 1988.

51. Story by Margaret Silf, based on a true story from the English Midlands.
52. Story by Margaret Silf.
53. Retelling by Margaret Silf of a story from *Wisdom in the Telling* by Lorraine Hartin-Gelardi, published by Skylight Paths Publishing, 2006.
54. Retelling by Margaret Silf of a traditional Iroquois legend.
55. Source unknown.
56. Source unknown.
57. Story by Margaret Silf.
58. Retelling of a traditional story, heard from Sharon Halsey-Hoover, from *Along the Water's Edge* by David Juniper, published by Paulist Press, 1982.
59. Story by Margaret Silf.
60. Story by Margaret Silf.
61. Story by Margaret Silf.
62. Story by Margaret Silf.
63. Retelling by Margaret Silf of a Native American story.
64. Story by Margaret Silf, based on the lyrics of a song by Margaret Scharf OP.
65. Story by Margaret Silf.
66. Retelling by Margaret Silf of a Russian story ("Death comes for the Aunt"), from *A Touch of Wonder* by Arthur Gordon, published by Fleming H. Revell/Baker Book House, 1974.
67. Story by Margaret Silf.
68. Story by Margaret Silf.
69. Retelling by Margaret Silf of a traditional Lakota story.
70. Story by Margaret Silf, based on a true story heard in Massachusetts.
71. Story by Margaret Silf, based on a story heard in Canada.
72. Story by Margaret Silf, inspired by an experience in Malaysia.
73. Retelling by Margaret Silf of a story from *The Song of the Bird* by Anthony de Mello, published by Doubleday New York, 1982.
74. Retelling by Margaret Silf of a story heard in Canada.

75. Source unknown.
76. Source unknown.
77. Retelling by Margaret Silf of a story from *Touching the Heart: Tales for the Human Journey*, by William J. Bausch, Twenty-Third Publications, 2007.
78. Story by Margaret Silf.
79. Retelling by Margaret Silf of a story heard in Ireland.
80. Retelling by Margaret Silf of a tale heard in central Europe.
81. Story by Margaret Silf.
82. Story by Margaret Silf.
83. Retelling by Margaret Silf of a story from *The Song of the Bird* by Anthony de Mello, published by Doubleday New York, 1982.
84. Retelling by Margaret Silf of an Ancient Greek legend.
85. Story by Margaret Silf.
86. Retelling by Margaret Silf of a traditional fable.
87. Source unknown.
88. Story of an incident encountered in KwaZulu-Natal, South Africa.
89. Source unknown.
90. Story by Margaret Silf, inspired by a story heard in Ireland.
91. Retelling by Margaret Silf of an Australian wisdom story.
92. Story by Margaret Silf.
93. Retelling by Margaret Silf of a traditional African tale.
94. Retelling by Margaret Silf of a Sufi story from *The Sufi Book of Life* by Neil Douglas-Klotz, published by Penguin Books, 2005.
95. Source unknown, but based on a retelling of a story from *Twelve and One-Half Keys* by Edward Hays, published by Forest of Peace Books, 1981.
96. Retelling by Margaret Silf of a Native American story.
97. Story by Margaret Silf, based on a true story heard in the USA.
98. Source unknown.
99. Source unknown.
100. Retelling by Margaret Silf of a British folk tale.

Don't miss Margaret Silf's original collection of Wisdom Stories...

This wonderful collection brings together one hundred wisdom stories from around the world. They spring from many different cultures, yet they speak a universal language. Arranged in sections that focus on different aspects of the human search for truth and meaning, this is a book to enjoy and inspire. It helps each of us discover our own story, and to live true to its wisdom.

978 0 7459 5541 4 | £9.99, US $16.95

69944301R00117

Made in the USA
Columbia, SC
18 August 2019